IN AN OPEN BOAT

A Journey from Poland to the Americas

Jerzy Tarasiewicz

OGAR PRESS   Tavernier, Florida

Photographs by

Dr. Czerwonka: p. 195, S. Mioduszewski: pp. 20, 22, J. Misiewicz: pp. 17, 78, 87, 101, 170. J, Tarasiewicz: pp. 2, 57, 122, 183, 208. L.Tremellat p 120. Unknown photographers: pp. 72, 73, 136.

Acknowledgments

All maps drawn by Ewa Tarasiewicz.

Very special thank you to my friend and editor, Gloria Vecsesi, and Andrew Stachiewicz for helping me with the graphics.

For information, write
OGAR Press • P.O. Box 933 • Tavernier, FL 33070

To my wife Ewa,

who was the reason for writing this book.

She said, "You will never do it."

About the author

Jerzy Tarasiewicz was born in Wilno, Poland, a graduate of Jagiellonian University in Krakow, and for two years he worked as a member of faculty there. He taught science in high school in the West Indies, then was a professor of physics at the University of Panama. He now lives with his wife in the Florida Keys, and they are summering in Maine.

CONTENTS

Chapter 14

Chapter 15

ILLUSTRATIONS

Illustrations

INTRODUCTION

"Jerzy Tarasiewicz and Janusz Misiewicz...after repairing an old life boat...went into THE UNKNOWN," words spare enough in one of my father's books, yet they are the presage to a feat of courage of two young men who chose to test the limits of a small life-boat in the most dangerous conditions at sea. However, the pages of *In an Open Boat* reflect more then that: they show what knowledge and physical prowess can achieve when the human mind and body are called upon to go almost beyond the limits of their possibilities.

The author of this work is a leader in this two-man team; though written with equanimity, the book leaves the reader in no doubt as to the skill and caring which Jerzy Tarasiewicz brings to bear on the relationship with his "crew" in all the most trying circumstances.

An expert sailor, and in years to come an outstanding physicist in the field of medical technology, Tarasiewicz is also a former journalist who demonstrates in his book a gift for the written word. As one winds through the pages, a sense of understated humor, warmth, and familiarity with the ever present danger become part of the reader's experience. The book is bound to appeal to anyone with a yen for adventure, but especially to those familiar with the sea and the vigilance and respect that it demands.

There are more things to come when, a few years later and as a graduate of the Jagiellonian University in Krakow, Tarasiewicz undertakes, with his wife Ewa, the formidable task of parting ways with the communist regime in Poland by carrying a sailboat across the Carpathian Mountains to the Mediterranean Sea and eventually landing on the shores of South America. But this is another story.

—*Danuta Borchardt*

1

Life on the lecture circuit.

---

*T*HERE WAS A TIME when I was on "lecture circuit" in Poland. My repertoire was monotonous; it was always about my crossing of the Atlantic in an open boat. I was paid handsomely—about 10 dollars per lecture. In communist Poland, 70 dollars per month was regarded as a very good salary.

After a while, I became quite proficient and knew how to handle a big crowd in a stadium, or a small audience in some club. After one of the more successful performances, in front of about two thousand people, there was a celebratory dinner with local notables, among them chief editor of the daily *Głos Koszaliński*. Near midnight a messenger from the editorial office came to the restaurant and handed a note to the editor. He read the message and said:

"Not in my newspaper!"

That way only *Głos Koszaliński*, of all the Polish communist party local dailies, did not publish an article declaring me an "enemy of the people."

Why have I suddenly become such a bad person? Almost two years before, when in London, I had written in the monthly published by Polish Merchant Marine Officers Organization in England, a piece about the situation in Poland. It had ruffled some feathers and ended my career as a crowd pleaser. At that time I was in the process of organizing an expedition, which was supposed to last about two years, employing a typical Baltic fishing boat about 75 feet long and modified into a schooner. We were supposed to sail around the world and describe fishing methods found in different places. Unfortunately this was also the end of that enterprise and therefore I cannot entertain you with the tale about how people fish in faraway places.

Ah, but the trip in an open boat did happen! Let me tell you how it was.

Puchatek *in Gotland.*

2

Why do it?—Trial voyage—Baltic storm—Gotland—Future plans.

W E HAD JUST GRADUATED from the Polish Maritime Academy, four of us, tight friends—Kazik Rywelski, Maryś Kosecki, and I—had known each other for many years preceding entrance to the academy. We had sailed together, joined Yacht Club Gryf in Gdynia while still in primary school. The fourth one, Janusz Misiewicz, became one of my best friends during the study. Young initiates, we were enthusiastic about the sea, about our future. Just about a decade after the second word war, was a time when stories about shipwrecked sailors were still very fresh. During these chaotic times after the war, ships were going down on stray mines or straying into then the still existing, marked minefields. Many aids to navigation were damaged or not reliable.

Radar was a novelty, ships were old and understaffed. A new generation of sailors did not have any experience in sailing on a small boat. The question how to behave once in a lifeboat was subject more to superstition than to science. Some people, for example Dr. Allen Bombard from France, had undertaken long voyages, trying to survive by drinking juice squeezed from caught fish, drinking salt water, etc. We were young, strong, well educated, with a vast experience in sailing small boats. We decided to do something about advancing knowledge on how to survive at sea. With the encouragement of our professors from the academy we proposed to take a standard lifeboat and sail her through storms in Northern Europe, the Bay of Biscayne, Northern Atlantic, and find the best methods to manage the boat safely.

There was another problem: psychological. Frequently the shock of leaving the big, comfortable ship for a small boat was enough to lose all hope, to give up. For that reason we decided to publicize our findings by the final stunt—crossing the Atlantic in that very same lifeboat.

Firstly we wanted to test the lifeboat (and ourselves) during a shorter trip on the Baltic Sea. For that trip we used a small 20 foot long boat, recently removed from one of the Polish merchant ships. Because the planned duration of the voyage was very short, about two weeks, not much work was necessary. We had to add only a new coat of paint and make sure the seams between the planks were tight. Everyone of the crew was an aficionado of Winnie the Pooh, therefore his was the name given to the boat: *Puchatek,* which is the way Poles translate the name of that brave bear.

Puchatek left Gdynia's yacht basin midday July 5, with a light easterly breeze. It was easy to keep course towards the eastern tip of Hel peninsula, about a 30 miles long sand spit sheltering the western part of the Gulf of Gdansk. We soon discovered that there was not one pencil on board. Near the shore of Hel a small coaster was lying at anchor, and a decision was made to ask its crew for a pencil. Pencil transferred, the officer of the watch asked where we were going.

"Visby, Gotland."

"Better wait here for a few days, a bad storm is coming."

"That suits us perfectly!"

Kazik, the oldest of the crew (and as long as I can remember looking older than his age), had been nicknamed "Dziadek," which means "Grandpa," was elected to be the cook. He prepared the first hot meal of the voyage—lots and lots of fried eggs.

At dusk the boat left the shelter of the peninsula and we were at open sea. While we were near the shore, a soldier of the Border Guard was trying to keep up with *Puchatek,* running on the sandy beach with his rifle, in a heavy overcoat. As a rule, soldiers of the Border Guard knew nothing about the sea or boats, heavily indoctrinated, seeing spies everywhere, terrified of their superiors, they could be dangerous. Some years ago, while on the engineless (that was the norm in those times), sizeable sailing yacht on which I was a crewman, we entered the port of Hel. With a strong northern wind we were attempting to moor at the eastern quay. A Border Guardsman was on the southern quay and was yelling to dock there. Seeing that the yacht was progressing in a "wrong" direction, he took his Kalashnikov and started shooting in the air. Our skipper decided to dock at the southern quay. The results were obvious: the swell in the harbor was causing our yacht to repeatedly, and heavily, hit the quay. The efforts of all eight members of the crew to keep her away were for nothing, and our port side was heavily damaged. After some time we were able to rouse the crew of a tug boat (it was Sunday) and we were towed to the eastern quay where temporary repairs were made and we could limp back to Gdynia.

One more of many instances was that of Captain Niedzielko—quite a famous sailor. While in command of the schooner *Zew Morza,* he was maneuvering the big boat, under sail, already inside the breakwater.

"Immediately bring the boat here!" yelled the very young Border Guardsman. Captain Niedzielko was doing just that; however, it was too slow for the soldier, who then let go a burst from his automatic pistol through the sails. Captain Niedzielko was a big man probably 250 pounds, well over 6 feet tall, with a great full beard. Because of his bulk, while moving his puffing was a good approximation of a steam engine. He docked

Zew Morza, disembarked, an image of fury, eyes bulging, he started to walk towards the terrified shooter. When he was close enough to reach the Kalashnikov, he grabbed it and pulled it from the soldier's hands, walked to the nearby guardhouse; the soldier, minus Kalashnikov, close behind him. Captain Niedzielko handed the gun to the very concerned officer, emerging from the guardhouse.

"Lock up the son of a bitch; he let me take his weapon!"

Puchatek was moving fast offshore, it was getting darker, soon we lost the view of "our" soldier. In a few hours it started raining, lightly in the beginning then harder and harder. The wind was getting stronger, waves began to break over the board of the boat. We had to shorten the sails. Then we dropped the mainsail, soon we had to reef our minuscule mizzen. It did not take long before a full gale was blowing. When the short night ended, we found ourselves at sea that was white with foam, the air was full of salt water spray, visibility was practically nil. All this time we were sailing under reefed mizzen and a very small jib. The boat was behaving better than anyone of us ever had expected. The fact that we could carry some sails gave us steerageway, we could more or less keep our course, and more importantly we could take the waves at the proper angle to avoid their breaking over the boat. Most of them, that is. In this kind of weather cooking was out of question, of course. Not everyone was up for eating, anyhow. Poor Maryś moved to the bottom of the boat, oblivious of the surroundings and the few inches of water sloshing around him. Janusz and I did not feel too well but we still could carry our share of the work without any problem, while Dziadek blessed with an iron stomach was in perfect shape.

The second night was the same; and the next night did not bring any relief. We started to have concern about Maryś; he could not hold any food nor drink. The rest of us ate some canned meat and Dziadek developed a concoction consisting of condensed milk and instant coffee; the sugar in the condensed milk gave us some energy, caffeine in the instant coffee kept us awake. We kept 2 hour watches, but steering was very tiring indeed, so we changed to 1 hour watches. One of us was steering, another one was on standby, tending to sails if needed, from time to time bailing out accumulated water. The third could have some cat naps, if he could.

Our third day was similar, more or less. Fortunately Maryś was slightly better. Dziadek prepared a mixture of grain alcohol and sweet cherry syrup and administered this to him in very small doses. That revived Maryś to such a degree that he could change his totally soaked clothes for something not exactly dry, but for sure much more comfortable. At dawn of the fourth day of the storm, the weather had started to change. The sun came out from behind the clouds, the wind started to die. We added more sail, but soon it was totally calm. The swell left by the storm was rocking our boat and the sails were flapping furiously, there was no reason to keep them up.

Dziadek, who took his duties as a cook very seriously, prepared a good hot meal; again there were four of us to run the boat. After four stormy days, when we did not have any chance to establish our position, our dead reckoning was doubtful. Measuring the elevation of the sun above the horizon during culmination gave us the exact geographical latitude. It was not difficult, we had our standard "mechanical" watches, we knew the approximate time of culmination, and it was enough to check when the sun had stopped to ascend. Simple calculations determined that we were close to the latitude of the southern tip of Gotland. But how far east or west off it? We had a crank-propelled radio transmitter and receiver tuned to the emergency wavelength. The same frequency was used to "raise" the desired radio station. It was always busy, ships were calling each other or land stations, land stations were trying to connect with the ships. To the untrained ear it sounded as an uninterrupted noise, consisting of Morse dots and dashes. If somebody would send an emergency signal SOS it could get lost in that noise. Because of that, "silence time" was established, starting on the hour and half past each hour, for three minutes, emergency wavelength could be used only for emergency communication.

We started our apparatus, waiting for the silence. The cut of signals was not clear; a few stragglers were still trying to take advantage of almost no traffic and were calling. On the other hand, the end of the period of silence was marked, within about two seconds of first Morse ti-ta-ti the ether was busy with tens of radios on the air. We did this procedure three times and, assuming that this gave us almost exactly the correct time, we took sight of the sun and found *Puchatek's* position. We were slightly to the east of Gotland. Next day we did the same, and found ourselves a few miles away from the previous day's position. Calm was complete, the sea was as smooth as a mill pond. We hoisted the sails, but the occasional little puffs of air could hardly move our boat.

We had stored our fresh water in two wooden casks of the standard issue for lifeboats. During the storm, a stopper of one of the casks was lost. How this happened would be difficult to say, maybe someone did not replace it properly, whatever. The important fact was that some salt water entered the cask and its contents became brackish. This was not an emergency, the water in the Baltic Sea is much less salty than the water in the oceans. This is especially true in its northern part, far from the Danish Straits leading to the Kategatt. Water with such a small salt content can be drunk safely, we have tried it—sweetened with condensed milk it was not too bad.

The seventh night at sea brought a light breeze and the following day we made to the little fishing port of Herta. After replenishing our fresh water supply we moved north along Gotland's eastern shore. It was difficult to refuse the temptation to land on the beautiful, tiny island, Ostergarn. Traveling in a flat bottomed boat was advantageous in that we could land practically on any sheltered rocky beach where water was only inches deep.

We encountered a day of head winds, and waited for a change in the port of Slite, then entered the strait between Gotland and Faro lying farther north. Entering the strait at dawn, we were halted by a patrol boat of the Swedish Navy. Unknown to us, Faro Island was a naval base. The Swedes did not want a boat flying the flag of a communist country next to their military installation, but the sailors were aware of our trip and quite accommodating. (It was wrongly assumed that we could not survive the storm and the Polish authorities asked all the ships in the region to be on the lookout for the remains of *Puchatek*. After Herta we were "found.") Nevertheless the Swedes' orders were to take us out of there. They towed us through Farosund, letting us go on the western side of Gotland and in a few hours we were in the capital of Gotland, Visby.

Visby is a beautiful, medieval city. It has plenty of relics from the time when it was a Viking base, and from the later times when it was a busy port, the most important one of all the Hanseatic League cities, even had a mint which struck their own money. At the end of the thirteenth century Swedes conquered Gotland, next came the Danes, then it became a base for pirates who terrorized Northern Europe in the fifteenth and sixteenth centuries. Finally it became a small, insignificant town. Even now, when it is an important tourist center, there are more ruined churches than those in use. Ruins of medieval fortifications, castles, churches are well exposed, spectacularly lit at night.

There we spent three days and on the sixteenth of July we left for the return trip. Again we could not resist the temptation to land on Lila Karslo, a small island next to the Western shore of Gotland. What intrigued us was the enormous quantity of sea birds. The wildlife officer met us on the shore and explained that Lilla Karslo was the equivalent of a wildlife refuge. He was very courteous and guided us to the more interesting places. The birds were tame, they did not show any fear of humans.

On the seventeenth of July, about eight in the morning the southern tip of Gotland was abeam. The eighteenth, at 8 PM we were south of Hel, in the Gulf of Gdansk. It was a pleasant, fast (for the lifeboat) trip, with strong northern wind. We have covered a distance of about 150 nautical miles in 36 hours, which gave us the speed of slightly more than 4 knots. Later on, we found that this was and still is, the top speed for this kind of craft.

The Gulf of Gdansk welcomed us with a dense fog and variable light winds. Finally, at 5 in the morning, we moored at our place in the Gdynia yacht basin. This was the end of the first step of our adventure. All four of us declared our commitment to participate in the voyage across the Atlantic, two years later.

3

Navy boot camp—m/s Piast—*Preparations*—
Dar Pomorza—*Departure.*

---

*A*FTER *PUCHATEK'S* RETURN we had to spend time in the
boot camp, at the Navy base at Ustka, a small harbor on
the Baltic Sea. During the years in the Maritime Academy, we
were forced to join the Polish equivalent of the American
ROTC. We knew that the Polish Navy was in need of navigation officers for its growing fleet of small submarines. The
idea of being forced into the Navy, and worse still to serve
on a submarine, did not appeal to me at all. Not only to me.
A few friends and I had decided to develop serious problems
with Navy officers running our Navy Reserve Officers program. We were infuriating them by showing total disrespect,
talking back, making sure that our grades in that program
were just "passing." Finally we managed to get two weeks of
brig time, the highest punishment available to the students.
That time was to be served during the Easter holiday.

We were assembled for the march to the brig, about 2 miles.
After checking that everyone was present, the commanding
officer read us the order of Commander-in-Chief of the Polish
Navy. It stated that because of the approaching "Day of the
Navy" we were given amnesty. We were crestfallen; all our
scheming was for nothing! After meaningful pause he added,
"But this punishment will be entered into your personal record!"

What a relief! We got what we wanted, on top of everything we did not have to waste 2 weeks of the spring vacation.

That affair took place a few months ago. It was impossible to skip boot camp, which was supposed to last four months, then we would be placed on the waiting list for a suitable ship to sign in. When we were "making ourselves comfortable" (what a misnomer!) in the barracks, the duty officer inquired if anybody was familiar with woodworking because some repairs were necessary. My friend Rysiek Kornacki and I were accomplished makers of ship models; we had been practicing that hobby for years. One thing we have learned during our limited (thanks God!) military training, that it is good advice to be apart from the crowd. Immediately we volunteered our services, taking Janusz with us.

The woodworking shop was very well equipped, so we decided to try to use our model-maker talents to ease the rigors of the boot camp. All our officers and non-commissioned officers were wearing Navy uniforms, but they were Army personnel, a bothersome fact for them which they tried to hide. When the duty officer was checking our work, I asked him if he would like to have a nice model of a warship. He took the bait, and we were excused for the time being of all the usual idiotic routine. Before we finished his model, other officers knew about our work, and his superior was next in line for another model. Then another. The last one was an unpleasant brute. Every day he checked our progress. We were working full time, but to make high quality model it takes weeks of diligent work. When the model was to be ready the following day, he announced that it would be our last day of model making—tomorrow we would join all the others and entertain ourselves by such activities as crawling in the mud, exercise on the parade grounds, etc. Then a horrible misfortune happened! Practically ready, the beautiful model of the historic destroyer *ORP Piorun*[1] fell from the table in such an unhappy manner that all the intricate details: masts, superstructure, a number of guns were broken! We were terribly sorry—the brute could not have his model on time. It took many days to repair the damage. In the meantime his superior had learned that it was possible to have a nice model for nothing, and we were safe. Higher ups were presented with models of the German pocket battleship *Deutschland* and the British aircraft carrier *HMS Ark Royal*.

We achieved a remarkable success—in four months we had rifles in our hands only five times. The first time when we received them, the second time when general quarters were called and we were force marching to "relieve the embattled friendly unit," the third time during another alarm when "our positions were under attack," the fourth time during the graduation ceremony and finally, the fifth time, when, as the freshly baked Naval officers (ensigns), we returned our rifles back to the Navy.

Only two of our colleagues were claimed by the Navy. They were sent to the Soviet Union to study in the Naval War College in Leningrad. Somehow they managed to be thrown out, and half a year later they were back in the merchant marine.

---

[1] *Piorun* found *Bismarck* on German's battleship's final night, and then with four other destroyers molested her until dawn. *Bismarck's* rudder was jammed; the destroyers kept her crew awake until everybody was completely exhausted. The German skipper was sure that the next day would bring the end to his battleship. Nevertheless he did not scuttle *Bismarck,* nor carry on an orderly "abandon the ship" procedure. During the morning battle with the British forces, the Germans did not score a single hit. Out of 2400 German crew only 118 were rescued. The captain of another German battleship *Graf Spee* (the sister ship of *Deutschland*), when surrounded by superior forces, scuttled her off of Montevideo, and the crew was rescued. Knowing what kind of welcome he would receive in Germany, he shot himself.

Within a month I signed onto a beautiful, fast boat, *m/s Piast*. She was a refrigerated ship on the South America line, carrying grapes, apples and pears from Patagonia; meat from the Argentinean pampas; and bananas from Brazil to the West European ports. From Europe we carried machinery, ceramics, electronics, etc.

After graduation from the Maritime Academy—we were not yet merchant marine officers—we signed on as "apprentices," something akin to hermaphrodite. We had to perform many of the sailor's chores: standing watch on a lookout or steering the ship, manning the winches when loading and unloading in the harbors not equipped with proper shore facilities, preparing the ship for the sea. We served as duty officers when in harbor, helping the chief officer with paperwork concerning the cargo, correcting the charts—normally a duty of the navigation officer—making frequently scheduled inspections of lifeboats, which was the duty of a third officer, standing on the bridge during maneuvers—otherwise the duty of an assistant. As a rule, when an apprentice was on board, the position of an assistant was vacant. It was an excellent training program.

To tell the truth, for me it was much more than that. During my school days, I spent five months as a trainee on a merchant vessel. Those days still were the "hard" communist days. The captain was a Navy man who did not know much about the sea. His previous duties were to rid the Polish Navy of pre-Second World War officers. He was rewarded with the command of *m/s General Walter,* a communist general, of course. The name of the ship was changed. She was previously named after the Polish city Biała. The captain was not trusted, as every captain[2] of sea-going vessels, he had

---

[2] In the communist countries.

a "second in charge." Our "second in charge" was a communist who was accused by the other communists of not being a good communist. After being "persuaded" to be a good communist, he was a mental wreck. Then someone else higher up took charge, and he was "rehabilitated." His rehabilitation was well rewarded financially by the present position on the *General Walter*. No one wanted to be close to him, save one sailor, who was the only Communist Party member among the whole crew, besides the captain and first officer, and of course close to nobody in the crew. This sailor's mental capability was probably higher than that of a capuchin monkey, but not by much. Even his soul mate, "second in charge," could hardly stand his presence.

While visiting a foreign port, we had to go ashore in teams of three. Then the "second in charge" would hold a meeting and all the horrible facts about capitalism were presented to us by the monkey brain sailor, or by brain blank rehabilitated communist.

During the *Piast's* voyages the situation was different. We had total freedom while at foreign ports; the position of the "second in charge" was abolished. Almost all the officers were well-trained graduates of the Maritime Academy. Only the first officer was an ex-Navy man. Every time he saw me on the bridge (which would mean about five times a day), he would volunteer his opinion. "Is it not true Mister Puchatek, that all this Maritime Academy is for nothing. Just two triangles: a plane for navigation and a spherical for astronavigation." I discovered a lot of communist propaganda leaflets stored in pantry. Once, after dinner, I read one of the leaflets in a way totally unintended by an author—putting the emphasis where it was not intended, changing the pronunciation, which in Polish could change the meaning. The final result was a mess room full of sailors rolling with laugher. There was a ton of this communist waste paper. Whenever something really stupid was discovered (an easy task), it was read for general amusement. Twenty seven days from Gdynia to Buenos Aires passed in merriment.

Then it was fall of the next year. As we had agreed after the Baltic trials, we disembarked from our ships and started preparing for the "Big Voyage." Unfortunately, "Grandfather" Kazik became seriously sick and could not take part in our enterprise. Maryś resigned as well, for whatever reasons, but taking into account his experiences in *Puchatek* we did not hold it against him, and we remained on friendly terms for many years after. Nevertheless, it was only up to the two of us to prepare an expedition. There was no lack of a bevy of volunteers. We decided that we would rather take a chance on only two of us, well trusted friends, than to try someone else.

The *Puchatek's* trip was well known among Polish sailors. Therefore it was no surprise that we practically lost our family names; on all four ships where we served our "apprenticeships" we were not called Mister Misiewicz, Mister Rywelski, or Mister Tarasiewicz, but simply—Mister Puchatek. We did not mind it, as a matter of fact we enjoyed it, it was a kind of tribute to our modest achievement on our small boat. From there it was a small step to name our next boat *Chatka Puchatków,* which could be translated as *Poohs' Hut.*[3]

We were given an old lifeboat from *m/s Batory,* built in 1936 in Italy, cedar planks on an oaken frame. She was thirty feet over all, ten feet four inches wide and was certified to hold seventy-two persons, but it would be difficult to sail her with more than twenty. For a long trip, taking into account the supply of food and water, a three person crew was the optimal

---

[3] *The House at Pooh Corner* is translated into Polish as *Chatka Puchatka.*

number. For a two person crew it was difficult to row, but we were accomplished oarsmen and could keep the course quite well, even without a helmsman. *Chatka Puchatków* had very fine lines (for a lifeboat); she was much finer than tub-like standard lifeboats of newer construction.

Under the benches there were watertight containers made of copper, they were filled with kapok fibers, which would assure flotation even in case the containers were damaged. The containers were equipped with watertight hatches about 10 inches in diameter. This arrangement allowed us to store some items, like charts, books, food items which were not in waterproof packages.

We had two suits of original sails, but we intended to use them only as heavy weather sails. For normal weather we made a slightly bigger mainsail and a jib. Lifeboats are notoriously difficult to steer under sail; they tend to pull to windward or to lee, depending on the apparent wind. For that reason, we added a small mizzen, which helped to keep the course with minimal rudder intervention.

Old lifeboat, the future Chatka Puchatków.

The library of the Maritime Academy was open to us; we could take whatever we needed: Sailing Directions, Nautical Almanacs, Lists of Lights, charts. At that time Polish Ocean Lines were getting rid of its older ships, mostly built in 1920s and 1930s. Also we had free access to the "used equipment" warehouses. Sextants, compasses, old-style kerosene navigational lights, barrels for storage of fresh water, etc., etc., all those important items we could have but for asking.

One chart was a problem: the chart of Martinique. We could not find it anywhere. Finally one of us remembered that our Maritime Academy training ship, the frigate *Dar Pomorza* had visited Martinique during one of her voyages, some twenty years ago. That day *Dar Pomorza* was lying at anchor about three miles offshore, well visible from the Yacht Club Gryf, a club to which I had belonged since I was ten years old and where we made our headquarters. It was a nice day with a strong westerly breeze; we took the club's wooden dinghy and soon we were at the gangway.

Captain Jurkiewicz remembered us well, it was only a few years earlier when, as the students of the second and third year of the Marine Academy, we had spent four months a year as cadets under his command. Captain Jurkiewicz was an extraordinarily strong man. Once, together with Maryś, in fine weather, we were repairing some of the rigging of the main lower topgallant sail. He was sitting astride the main lower topgallant yard. Nearby a team of cadets was trying to pull down one of the staysails. Captain Jurkiewicz, who was looking critically at that endeavor, decided that somebody forgot to slacken staysail's halyard. Furiously, he undid it and let it fly. Unfortunately the undone line was a halyard of the main upper topgallant sail. The topgallant yard sailed towards Maryś. Fortunately there was a breeze which slowed the descent of the yard, and Mary´s could duck. Captain Jurkiewicz saw his mistake and single-handedly hoisted the main topgallant sail, a feat that normally requires a team of five.

On another occasion, *Dar Pomorza* was caught in a very heavy storm, a few hundred miles southeast of the Azores. Confused waves had rocked the boat so hard that a heavy iron support of an aerial on the top of the mizzenmast was bent out of shape, shorted the aerial, and our radio station was muted. The storm lasted less than three days, but the seas remained so high that for two more days it was impossible to go to the top of the mast to do repairs. Finally, my very good friend Czesiek Frukacz and I, who had become the team used for the most intricate work in the rigging, decided to give it a try. To get to the top of the mast one had to use the Jacob's ladder, a quite inconvenient, narrow arrangement made of steel rungs attached to two steel cables. Standing on that ladder we tried to straighten the support, it did not work, we could not apply enough force. Finally, I perched myself on the top of the mast and while using my weight and taking advantage of the rocking of the boat, managed to straighten the damn thing. I was secured by the piece of line, but it was hairy. I noticed Captain Jurkiewicz, who all this time was observing our efforts, during this finale found something interesting on the deck to look at. After we climbed down, the watch officer commanded us to go to the captain's cabin. When we arrived there we found the captain, with his steward holding a tray burdened with two glasses of brandy, "to warm up" said the Captain.

One way or another, as I have said, Captain Jurkiewicz remembered us well. In minutes the map of Martinique was found, we were presented with it. Then a big surprise: on the spot I was offered position of the junior officer. It was a great honor, and besides that, by law, the time of service on the training ship was counted double towards a higher rank. Of course I could not leave Janusz after we had spent months in preparation for the voyage, nor did I myself like the idea of abandoning the *Chatka Puchatków* project. That vacant position went to the best man possible: Czesiek Frukacz.

Chatka Puchatków, *moored at the Yacht Club Gryf in Gdynia, a few days after being launched.*

It would be laborious to row against the wind, all the way to the Yacht Club. Fortunately one of the ship's boats was being readied for the trip ashore and we traveled fast behind her, on the tow line.

After all, why were we so concerned about Martinique? We could attempt to land on any West Indian island. True, but Martinique has one great advantage, on its eastern point, more or less in the middle of the island, there is a very powerful lighthouse.[4] We anticipated that we could have some problems with establishing accurate longitude. In case we would be approaching land during the night (about a 50% chance), on the not very maneuverable lifeboat, we would like to have as much time as possible to steer towards the channel between the islands, away from the windward shore. We could calculate latitude very well, easily enough to reach channel, but what would happen in case we would pass the islands at night and woke up in the morning 20 or 30 miles in the Caribbean? We would then have to tackle against the trade wind and current for hours and hours, if not days.

After many bureaucratic delays we were ready to leave. Unfortunately it was already the eight of August, about five weeks behind our intended date of departure. A small crowd of well wishers (and customs officers and officials of the Border Guard) had gathered on the quay of Yacht Club Gryf, but we could not move. There was not a breath of wind. Finally a few friends sat at the oars of the dinghy and towed us behind a breakwater. Sails hoisted long ago found some

---

[4] Lighthouse La Caravelle Fl (3), 15 sec, range 22 nautical miles.

Chatka's *crew on the day of departure.*

very light breeze, light but enough for *Chatka* to move. We were quite tired—last minute preparations, the worry if by any chance some authority will not throw another unsigned paper in our way. *Dar Pomorza* was still at anchor, we dropped ours near by, and in such splendid company have spend our first night "at sea."

In late morning we were woken up by the boat from *Dar Pomorza*. They brought us some last minute gifts and wishes of strong winds. In no time the anchor was up, sails hoisted and we were on our way. Oarsmen from *Dar Pomorza* saluted us by lifting vertically their oars. We dipped our flag. That was our real departure.

4

First storm—Christianso—Svaneke—Falsterbo Canal—Kattegat—Skerries—Skagerrak—Norway— Horns Reef—The North Sea.

TWO DAYS LATER we had our first stormy weather, 8 on the Beaufort scale. The storm was of short duration, less than 24 hours. Whenever we could, we trolled a big fishing lure hoping to catch something fresh. It is difficult to hook and land a fish on a sailboat, very often there is not enough time to "stop" the boat and the fish is lost. The next morning after the storm was calm. I tried to catch some sleep, it was Janusz's watch, and he was trying to catch some fish. He woke me up by yelling, "I have it, I have a fish!" Surely, a big cod hooked itself. The fish, caught at great depth (boat was nearly stationary and the fishing line was going practically straight down) was suffering from the decompression and was hardly moving. Nevertheless, just next to the boat, the hook got loose and our cod slowly started to sink. I could not stand it, and I jumped overboard after the fish. The cod suddenly learned to swim again and escaped from my hands. Janusz commented that the splash I made was so big it would awaken a dead cod, not merely a stunned one. Those heroics were totally unnecessary; soon we had five decent size cod in the boat, the biggest almost two feet long.

The worst thing during a sailing trip is to hurry. Our plan was to spend some time sailing the familiar Baltic, to get well acquainted with the boat, to make corrections in the rigging, if necessary, to be ready for the "real" trials which we suspected were awaiting us on the more dangerous waters. But we were late, and we had to use whatever was left of the summer in a sensible manner. Entering Simrishamn was uneventful. During the day the breeze freshened a little, we were moored to the quay, the wind was pushing the boat against it, we were slightly concerned about it, but there was no apparent damage. The nearby harbor of the tiny archipelago Christianso looked difficult enough to be worth trying to enter. The wind was light and variable, we spent the whole day trying to reach the harbor, but whenever we were close, the wind changed, always in the wrong direction. Finally, near sunset, a strong breeze started blowing from WSW. We attempted to enter Christianso from the south; the harbor, actually a strait between two islets, can be entered from both directions. The southern passage is facilitated by the light displayed in sectors: red—too far to the left, white—safe sector, proceed, green—too far to the right. We did not take into account that a strong breeze blowing over the shallow water of the entrance will raise a nasty, steep swell. We were in the white sector, but *Chatka* could not stay on course, we were drifting, very fast, towards the windward shore of the eastern islet. The light changed to green. The shore was so close, that we could not see the light anymore, only glare on the clouds hanging low above steep-to shore. Anticipating trouble, we prepared two oars to be used as steering oars, one at the stern, another at the bow. Trouble was now. We dropped the sails, and working together we turned the boat, hoisted the sails and escaped the shore. The breeze freshened and we had a tough time hauling in the sheet of the mainsail. Of course we did not have time to reef the sail, but anyhow we wanted to have as much pulling power as possible, to get away.

Bornholm, a sizeable island, could offer us some protection from the rising wind and seas. If we kept sailing on the starboard tack, about 60 degrees off the wind, we could reach Svaneke. With every mile, sailing became more and more comfortable; just after sunrise we were securely moored in that little cozy harbor. To our surprise we had a lot of water in the boat. After close examination we discovered that the Simrishamn's battering had not been harmless, the boat had sprung a leak on the port side, along the waterline. We careened *Chatka* by tying a block and tackle between the top of the mizzenmast and a sturdy bitt on the shore. For that operation we added extra (temporary) shrouds to the mizzen mast. Everything went without a hitch, the loose packing was replaced, and the boat was again watertight. A few other changes were made: remembering how difficult it was to properly trim the main sail when we were escaping from Christianso, we changed the arrangement of the main's sheet, the double block was changed to triple. In the nearby forest we cut a few saplings to use as whisker poles for the boomless mainsail and jib. Canned food was stripped of its paper labels, greased to protect from corrosion, and packed in a systematic manner. We rearranged the position of other items: from our experience of seven days we knew what should be positioned where, to be most handy during the times when the weather did not cooperate. All that work took time, we have spent three days in Sveneke, but it was worthwhile.

On our way towards Skagerrak we had to pass near Christianso. Both of us were slightly stubborn (Janusz preferred the phrase "of strong character"). With a steady, strong wind it took us less than three hours from the time we left Svaneke to the moment when we were there. The harbor-strait is divided into the northern and southern part by a bridge linking two islets, Christianholm and Fridriksholm. Part of the population (120 permanent residents) was engaged in fishing, but it seems that the main occupation was to cater to tourists. Most of the tourists seemed to be of an artistic inclination; every so often there was someone with an easel, painting a local scene. Obviously, many moons ago, Christianso was an important base for a naval force. On both sides of the harbor heavy mooring rings were fastened to the rocks. When there was no bridge, ships could easily exit by the northern or southern entrance, whichever was favored by the wind blowing that day. Both islets are surrounded by a wall of loosely piled rocks; lots of cannons are positioned within. Further inland is a big blockhouse, of the same construction, again full of cannons. The lighthouse is situated on the top of an old tower. We climbed there and were rewarded by an incredible vista. Leaving the tower we tried to pay a small, rather symbolic entrance fee. The lighthouse keeper refused to accept it, he had observed our maneuvers three days ago and expressed the opinion that it was an act of "superior seamanship." Did we feel proud? You bet.

It seems that we had either too much wind, or not enough. Again, after leaving Christianso we were becalmed. But after a calm day we had some breeze from the east! We supplemented our standard suit of sails with staysails hoisted on shrouds, mainsail and mizzen were set wing and wing, and the boat was really moving. The wind freshened and veered a little towards north. It was time to reduce sail, first, down went the improvised additions, then we had to change the mainsail for the trysail. We were quite close to the shore and the seas were not high. Wind reached Force 10. Our speed over bottom, no doubt augmented by a drift current, had reached 8 knots, fantastic for a lifeboat. Cape Sandhammaren, with its big, white lighthouse erected on a sandy spit was behind us. It was still daylight, but there was so much spray in the air that visibility was not good and we saw the big, white lighthouse only as a misty silhouette. Just about sunset we passed Ystad, and two hours later, already in total darkness, Trelleborg.

The southwestern tip of Sweden is cut by the Falsterbo Canal; it reduces considerably the distance between the Baltic Sea and Kategatt. About an hour after Trelleborg, we identified the weak entrance lights to the canal. Because of quite common southwestern storms in this area, the entrance is protected by a sizeable breakwater, forming a spacious roadstead. Janusz was at the tiller, trying to get close to the windward, the eastern entrance tower with a green light. There was more open water here and the waves became higher. Janusz, concentrating on properly "taking" few bigger combers, went too far north; our boat was in an area where the entrance lights were obscured. We were prepared for this kind of a situation—a gun loaded with white parachute flare was handy. Launched, it revealed, in its ghostly light, the breakwater with huge seas breaking over the top, and most importantly for us, showed the position of the entrance. I jumped to the sheets of the mainsail, we had to jibe. Janusz steered to port and soon we could see the green and red entrance lights, changed our course to starboard, and minutes later we were behind the breakwater, well sheltered.

It took us most of the next day to pass the canal, but once we had left it we had a very favorable strong wind, sheltered waters, sailing on the starboard tack with the quartering wind, in a few hours we were in Copenhagen. According to the local custom we moored between four palings, bow toward the shore. *Chatka* was in the company of more than a thousand sailing boats of every kind and description. Somehow many of the Danish sailors knew about us, and we were welcomed in the most cordial manner. That evening, in an enormous clubhouse of the local yacht club, an enormous party was given. Before fun started, the commodore had a lot to say. The day was windy, squally, tens of yachts were on the water, and there were some mishaps. One boat suffered a broken mast, a few small boats had capsized, some sails were torn. Every one of those events was commented on by the commodore. Those skippers who had rushed to help the unlucky ones were praised and presented with small gifts. Those who were careless were reprimanded. The skipper of the boat near the one with the broken mast, who did not render immediate help was really scolded. All assembled were taking part in the proceedings, the hosts were thoughtful about our lack of understanding Danish, an interpreter was provided, and we could follow everything very well.

After a short stay in Copenhagen we wanted to visit Goteborg. This harbor is often visited by Polish merchant ships. We were extremely short of cash and, while meeting Polish vessels, we could always count on fresh provisions to replenish our pantry. In terms of Polish "zloty" (meaning "golden") we were quite well off, but restrictions governing the taking of foreign currency out of Poland were draconian (if you were not a member of the communist party insider). We were permitted to exchange our zlotys for 87 U.S. dollars. Why 87? I do not have any idea. For sure we had to guard our finances well.

During communist times, the crews of Polish yachts, when on the very rarely permitted trips that included landing abroad, were allowed to take with them only a minimal "quota" of "dewizy," that's how non-Polish currency was referred to in official parlance. This brings to mind the story of a group of Polish yachtsmen strolling in Stockholm. Their attention was drawn to the prices of items displayed in a store specializing in luxurious leather apparel. Full length overcoats were about 7 dollars, sport coats around 4. Short of cash as they were, this was too much, they entered the store and started to pick up the merchandise. To their surprise the staff was taking the items from their hands, and on top of everything in quite an unfriendly manner, telling them something in Swedish. The mystery was gone when someone speaking English arrived; the "store" was a chemical cleaning outfit specializing in leather goods.

The narrowest part of Little Sund, the strait leading to Kategatt, lies between Helsingor on the Danish side (site of Hamlet's castle) and Halsingborg on the Swedish coast. When we reached that part, the wind was practically gone. With a slight current going south, we decided to land in Helsingor and wait for a change in weather. The wait was not long, in a few hours we got a SW wind, and again we were on our way. The wind was growing stronger, that was all right with us, what we did not like was the dense fog, it came out of nowhere, just after passing the lightship *Lappe Ground,* changing a beautiful sunny day into a gray, wet, and cold. The night was miserable. This area is known for very heavy ship traffic. All around us we could hear sirens of many ships. We steered a little to the west, to be away from the main ship lane. Janusz was tooting on our little horn, it did not help me to have a restful sleep. When I took the watch, my music did not help him to rest either. Three short blasts every minute, sometimes more often, when more signals were about us, or when someone was too near us for comfort; three short blasts mean "a sailboat is running downwind"; we changed the course slightly towards the east, to get a fix on the lightship *Kattegat S.* It was not a pleasant situation: we could not use landmarks to establish our position, the fog was too dense to see anything farther than a hundred feet. The moon was near full, it made the night less dark, but forget about seeing the moon itself, to say nothing about seeing the horizon. Dawn came, hardly noticeable. Finally I could hear the fog horn of *Kattegat S.* Louder and louder. Suddenly here she is! Her blurred shape appeared to hang just above *Chatka.* It was only an illusion, with our four knots we had ample room to avoid collision, to change the course towards Anholt (an island a few miles long in the middle of Kategatt) our next milestone before entering the skerries in the vicinity of Goteborg. Another few hours and it was the end of the nasty fog, another pleasant day of sailing.

About twenty miles south of Goteborg begins an extensive field of skerries, a multitude of small islets. Some of them measure half a mile, some are big enough to sport one tree. In this area tides are still minuscule (in the Baltic Sea they are nonexistent), and on many skerries there are vacation houses, some shacks, some mansions. Quite often deep water comes next to shores of those islets. All together it is a very picturesque region. One can assume that Swedes are very protective of those beauties. Incredible amounts of navigational lights are situated in that maze, for obvious reasons—to prevent anybody to ram any of their skerries. We entered that strange "intercoastal" route to Goteborg at the end of a short, northern night. The moon was hanging low, we could vaguely see the outline of islets. Red, green, and white lights were blinking everywhere. Navigation was child's play, the weather just right—strong southerly wind, no seas higher than a foot in those protected waters. Our expedition had some serious goals: how to manage a lifeboat in difficult and varied conditions, but after all we were sailors at heart, from time to time we loved to enjoy a good and pleasant sail. Among the skerries of Goteborg we got one. Soon it was sunrise. The big red orb of the sun appeared above the eastern horizon. The big red orb of the moon was gracing the western sky. A cacophony of navigational lights was still visible. In that fairyland we made port in Goteborg.

We moored a little west of the commercial harbor. We wanted to keep close to the Kategatt, to be able to leave harbor whenever conditions would be right. Aboard *m/s Pilica,* Captain Franckowiak, was taking cargo in Goteborg. As usual, we received a most pleasant welcome, not to mention fresh supplies. Again on Kategatt. Sailing was easy, but unfortunately slow. We could rest, but that was not our intention, even the Northern Lights illuminating for hours the nightly sky could not remove from our minds the important fact—it was the beginning of September, we were late. The fourth of September was a gala night: first the Northern Lights were most spectacular, then shortly after midnight a brightly lighted passenger liner appeared. We were close enough to be sure that it was the Polish liner *m/s Batory.* We knew that on this voyage she was under the command of Captain Meissner, our professor of navigation in the Maritime Academy, our sponsor of the present voyage! Unfortunately, that night we could not establish contact with *Batory.* During the display of the Northern Lights the sea around us was on fire, fluorescence was so great that it was illuminating the inside of our boat. Were those two phenomena related? Were all those tiny organisms in the seawater fooled into "answering" the signals of Northern Lights? The fluorescence died when Northern Lights disappeared.

The next two days of calm. A strong current had moved us 40 miles in 22 hours, far to the north, we were at 58 degrees 50 minutes northern latitude. Never anticipating reaching those waters, there were no charts of this region on board of *Chatka.* We had to improvise, after drawing the Mercator grid on the reverse of one of our charts, we plotted the positions of lighthouses taken from the publication *List of Lights.* Using that skeletal chart we entered the small Norwegian port of Risor. After stretching our legs, we tried to sail south, using the light sea breeze, keeping inside fjords. When we had to exit into the open Skagerrak, again it was calm.

In this region the current has southerly direction and flows quite fast. The next night, the ninth of September, we could see the blinking of the lighthouses on the northern shore of Jutland. With the morning light we could see the tops of trees growing in Hanstholm; we were near the northwestern tip of Jutland. Towards midday the wind came from the northern direction, we should welcome it, but we knew that it was a precursor of a strong storm from the northwest. We did everything, weather permitting, to move as far west as possible. We were too close to the land to hove to, soon the waves became so large that we could steer only about south by west. Night came and our eastern horizon was lit by the Danish lighthouses. We could easily take bearings on those lights, and we could easily determine that our true course was practically due south.

About sixty miles south from Hanstholm, near the cape Blavands Huk, starts the tongue of shallows of Horns Reef. It projects west for about 30 miles, with the minimum depth of about 12 feet at low water. Twelve feet is more than enough water for *Chatka Puchatków,* but it was blowing more than 35 knots and the average waves were about 20 feet high. There was no question in our minds: waves must be breaking heavily on the Horns Reef. It did not make sense to beach the boat on the beaches of western Jutland. To reach the shore we would have to cross the line of breakers, with the wind blowing about 45 degrees to the shoreline, the surf would be quite confused, conditions would be no less dangerous than on the Horns Reef. We knew the time of high water (it was early in the morning) and then the depth would be greater and the surf should be smaller. Already we were carrying only our storm jib, about four square feet. To slow the boat even more we would have to run under bare poles, but then we would not be able to keep our southern course. At three in the morning, during Janusz's watch, I had managed to get a good fix, we were about 20 miles offshore, about 20 miles north from Horns Reef. Nothing to be done, I ducked into the nest of spare sails and went to sleep. Nominally I was the skipper, but Janusz's ability to handle the boat was comparable to mine, it was a great comfort. Dozing on and off on the tossing boat I could hear the roar of the breakers skillfully "taken" by Janusz. Some salt spray that from time to time hit the canvas, did not bother me at all.

Finally, at about eight in the morning, already on my watch, we saw in front of *Chatka* the breakers of Horns Reef. It looked like a mass of foam; we could also see particular breakers moving from the northwest, and to our surprise from the northeast. No question therefore, the surf was very confused, using the sea anchor was very iffy, and we made the decision to surf under sail. A steering oar was ready, but the boat was answering to the rudder very well, besides steering with the tiller I could sit more securely in the sheets of the stern. Janusz was next to the mainmast, ready to work our tiny jib. The one thing I had to worry about was that a big wave might throw the rudder from its hinges. The rudder was secured by the stout line to the boat, but it would be impossible to make any repairs under these conditions. I elected to use the tiller, pushing it down with my weight, and have a steering oar as a standby. The first big breaker of the surf came. No problem. Then the second, from a ninety-degree direction different from the first—we were jibing, Janusz threw the jib to starboard, we did not have to say a word (which probably in the roar of the breakers would have been inaudible), both of us knew exactly what to do. A few more "standard" breakers, then, we first heard and then saw, in the air full of spray, a monster. Much, much higher than any before, it appeared to approach us slowly, we were "escaping" from it under our jib and poles.

I steered perpendicularly to the wave, got a lot of speed sailing "downhill," and, seeing that its head was already broken to our starboard, I steered the boat to windward. In seconds we were in the foam, just slightly in front of its highest point. Because the foam is light, the boat was sitting very low, we were immersed in the foam, the foam was pouring into the boat along its total length on both sides. With that high speed I could keep our boat in the desired position with minimal movement of the rudder. We were already in that position, the idea was not to lose it, to stay with the broken wave until we would reach quieter waters. To lose the breaker would make it necessary to play with other big waves, which is always tricky. While on the rear slope of a breaker, a boat may lose her speed, she will not answer the rudder, and can be "breached," and if the situation is not corrected in time, she can be swamped, or worse, capsize. By minutely changing the angle of the boat to the breaker, it is often possible to keep surfing for a long period. Soon "our" wave started to flatten out, instead in foam we were on water. The ride was short, probably less than a minute; a lot of the foam that fell into the boat brought little water, slightly more then ten buckets. Before the first breaker I glanced at my watch, after the "ride" I looked again. The whole passage of Horns Reef took less than five minutes.

Horns Reef forms some kind of underwater breakwater. The seas were much smaller, a few hours later the wind subsided considerably, we hoisted more sails. We had passed Horns Reef, we were on the North Sea, we had not suffered any damage to our boat, nor to our egos.

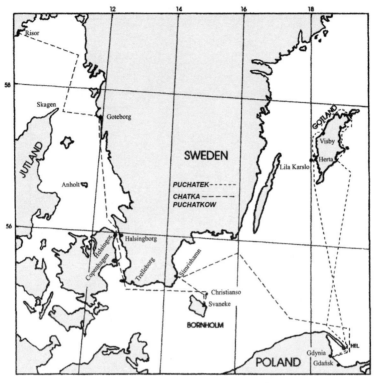

The course of Puchatek *Gdynia-Visby-Gdynia and*
Chatka Puchatków *from Gdynia to Risor.*

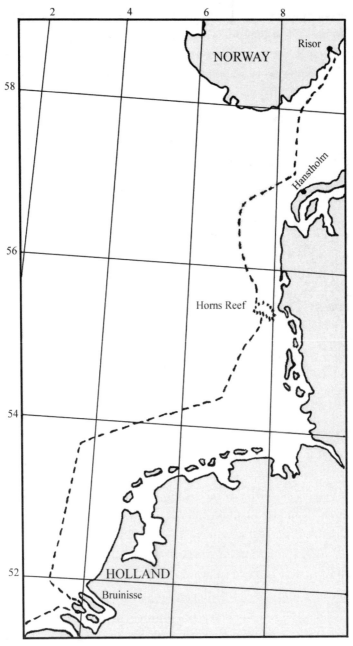

The course of Chatka Puchatków *from Risor to Bruinisse.*

5

Guest book in Grenada—Our hometown Wilno—Sailing the North Sea—White squall—Dutch waters—Ostend—Dunkirk—Maritime Academy—Bethune—Goodwin Sands—Dunkirk again.

---

*D*URING ONE OF MY VOYAGES, while on the West Indian island of Grenada, I was the guest of Dr. Słonimski, a Polish physician and an enthusiastic yachtsman. Grenada, with its numerous safe harbors is one of the places most favored by the sailors in West Indies. In his home, Dr. Słonimski kept a guest book; during more than twenty years of residency on Grenada he had accumulated an impressive collection of signatures of many yachtsmen, some more famous and some less famous, but most of them had sailed for a long time and completed beautiful passages. While he was showing me the book, he carried a running commentary about boats and their crews. Quite a few of the comments sounded like this: "Shipwrecked on Santa Margarita Island," "Shipwrecked in the Cook Islands," "Fell overboard near Durban and was never found," "Lost at sea."

Let us remember, books about long voyages in small boats most often describe successful voyages.

We passed through Horns Reef in the morning of September 11, the weather was improving, and we were adding more and more sails. First the mizzen, then changing the storm jib for a working sail, then the double reefed main for the main with single reef, then just before nightfall for a full suit of working sails. Next day gave us pleasant sailing weather, we could rest, cook a good meal, have some conversation, relive recent adventures, congratulate ourselves.

You have probably noticed that our family names end in "ewicz." Before the Second World War this would indicate strongly that we were from the eastern part of Poland, most probably from Wilno. This was the case here, we were both born in Wilno, just as our parents. After the Second World War, when Stalin was permitted to take a big part of Eastern Poland, millions of Poles were moved west, among them our families. Janusz's settled in Łódź, in central Poland, mine in Sopot, a small town between Gdańsk and Gdynia, two sea-ports on the coast of the Baltic Sea.

Originally the Wilno region was a part of Lithuania and Rus.[5] After 1386 when Lithuanian Grand Duke Jagiello married the Polish Queen Jadwiga, both countries shared the kings, then in 1569 Lithuania and Poland became one country, united in the celebrated Union of Lublin. Culturally Wilno had a mixture of Poles, Belarussians and Lithuanians. Long before the Grand Duke Jagiello, Belarussian has become an official language of the Great Duchy of Lithuania. It is very similar to Polish[6] and is written both in the Cyrillic and the Latin alphabet.

---

[5] Present day Belarus, which means White Rus, to differentiate from Ruś Czerwona (Red Rus), further south. Those historical names have nothing to do with "White Russians" and "Red Russians," anticommunist and communist fractions during civil war in Russia, following the First World War.

[6] "Usie ludzi naradzajutsa svabodnymi i rounymi u svajoj godnasci i pravach"—Belarussian.

"Wszyscy ludzie rodza sie swobodnymi i rownymi w swojej godnosci i prawach"—Polish.

"All human beings are born free and equal in dignity and rights"—English.

Inhabitants of the Wilno region have developed quite a distinct accent, easily recognizable, incorporating more of the singsong pronunciations of Belarussians. Some other ethnic groups have joined this frontier society. For example, according to family tradition, my forefathers were descendants of a Tartar bey, a chief of a group of Tartar warriors who fought on the side of Jagiello in 1410, and helped to win the great battle with the Teutonic Knights, not far from Grunwald. He was knighted in 1414 and given an estate west of Wilno.

In 1939 Russia and Germany divided Poland among themselves. In 1940 Russia annexed Lithuania,[7] proclaimed it Soviet Socialist Republic, part of the Soviet Union. The Polish lands taken by the Soviets in 1939 were divided between the Soviet Socialist Republics Belarus, Ukraine and Lithuania. Severe repression of the Polish culture followed, Lithuanian communists and their Russian masters were trying to stamp out the Polish intelligentsia. My father (a surgeon) and one of my uncles (an engineer) took cover working as "pilshchyki," hiring themselves as the cutters of firewood. Another of my uncles, who was taking part in defense of the naval base, Oksywie, near Gdynia, managed to escape from a German POW camp and arrived in our family house. He was born in Wilno and knew it as a Polish city. On his arrival all the signs were in Lithuanian, among others "Kierpikła," "Mokikła." When a streetcar was ready to go, the conductor would call "ważojem." To call somebody's attention on the street, people were shouting "pałaj, pałaj." My uncle, lighthearted and fun loving, put those words to a popular melody and during dinners entertained us by singing it, then rang the bell of my tricycle, called "ważojem"; it was a signal to drink another

---

[7] As well as Latvia and Estonia.

toast. He told us some war stories. During the battle of Oksywie, he discovered a German sniper, not far away, who was taking aim at my uncle. According to him, he could see the bore of the German's rifle as a circle. Since he was a good shot, he managed to shoot the sniper first. My grandmother's reaction was, "How could you do it? To kill a human being?"

"It was I or the German, what should I have done, mother?"

Many illustrious personages have hailed from that frontier region: Henryk Sienkiewicz, who received the Nobel Prize in literature, Adam Mickiewicz, one of the greatest Polish poets. Also Captain Jurkiewicz, the commandant of *Dar Pomorza,* and countless others. We felt very proud to belong to that group; many of our actions were dictated by that pride.

The next night, the twelfth of September, our southern horizon was ablaze with the glare of lighthouses on the Dutch coast. We could easily identify them, without seeing the actual light. We were fifty miles offshore, far behind the theoretical visibility. It happens quite often; after stormy weather comes a short period of incredible good visibility. Many, but not all data of the lighthouses can be found on the nautical charts. For example, how strong is the source of the light? How long is a flash? A light of the same intensity, but accumulated in a short flash it will appear brighter and its glare will be visible farther. How tall is the tower? A chart will show only the elevation above the sea level. Knowing the type of construction—masonry tower, steel framework, etc.—will help identify the lighthouse during the daytime. The way a lighthouse is painted (if it is painted), other descriptions, for example "cupola on the old red brick tower," could be helpful, especially when approaching land in bad visibility. All that information is listed in the *List of Lights.*

We were sailing far offshore but, typically for the North Sea, the water was shallow; on our position there was less than one hundred feet. A light breeze was pushing us ahead, but we knew that at this time the tidal current was in the contrary direction to our course. Janusz dropped the lead line, it was pointing forward, the current was faster than our speed on the water; he dropped the anchor, it caught the bottom. If not a taut anchor line, *Chatka* had all the appearances of sailing slowly southward, she was rocking gently, behind her stern was a wake, and not a scrap of land in sight. In a few hours the tidal current changed its direction, we weighted the anchor and the boat was again sailing south, this time helped by the current.

During the night of 14 and 15 September, we were surrounded by big, dark clouds, and we could see intensive lighting in every direction. A confused swell was coming seemingly from everywhere. We remembered similar weather, very close to the present position, during our stint on *Dar Pomorza*. Fortunately it was near the sunset, and it happened that two watches were present on deck for changeover at eight bells.[8] A squall hit with great force, the big ship's leeward gunwale was underwater. Two helmsmen[9] were given the order to go hard to lee, but before the ship was on course before the wind, a number of lighter sails, some upper royal

---

[8] Normally at 8 bells (4 double rings), 12, 4, and 8 AM and PM there is a change of watch. A half an hour later there would be a single ring of the ship's bell, at the full hour one double ring (two bells), and so on. In that system every sailor would have to serve during the same time each day and night (for example, "graveyard watch" midnight to four in the morning). In order to avoid that, sometimes one four-hour period is divided into two-hour watches, that way every day everyone serves during different hours. It seems more just, but it is difficult to get used to this "moving" bedtime.

[9] *Dar Pomorza* had a traditional steering system, without power assistance. She had two coupled steering wheels, each could be manned by two sailors. During normal weather only one wheel was manned.

topsails and some lower royal topsails were in shreds flapping furiously, there was the danger that we could lose the wooden upper yards. In no time a number of us were in the rigging, on the yards, cutting off the remnants of damaged sails, sending them into the squall driven rain in front of the boat.

We did not take any chances, almost all sails were down, what we hoisted were only small storm sails in order to be able to maneuver the boat when and if we would be hit by a squall. In terms of forward progress this did not make any difference; we were in a calm, as I had mentioned, a swell was murderous, our small sails were flapping furiously. A strong wind came only in the morning, after sunrise. It blew from SSW, near gale, about 7 on the Beaufort scale. Despite short, nasty seas, we were keeping to southeast, to get some shelter from the still invisible land. About 1 PM Janusz saw the lightship *Georee,* and not more than two hours later we entered the passage between two Dutch islands. While approaching land, we met on the water a number of Dutch fishermen. What they saw was a lifeboat, and they assumed that we did not know the local waters. Every person, on every boat we saw, got up, raised his arm and with small up and down motion pointed towards the passage between shallows.

We did not intend to call at any Dutch port, so we did not carry exact charts of those waters. We just wanted to spend a night in some small harbor, but we could not see any; for two hours of proceeding inland all we saw were enormous levies. Finally there was an open lock in a levy. When we were closer, a great surprise: a car was driving through this lock! Obviously it was closed only during a dangerous storm surge, normally it afforded an access to the shore. We were in tidal waters, but the tide was high, and we noticed a small channel marked by tree branches stuck in the mud. Following it, we found ourselves in some kind of recreational pool, people were swimming, small boats were moored to its sides. A number of people there could speak English, and when asked if there was any nearby "real" harbor, they directed us to the other side of the island, to the small port of Bruinisse. It was getting late, the wind was dying, and we made Bruinisse well after dark, about ten o'clock. When asking for the Harbor Master, we were directed to a private house, there we found the Harbor Master with some friends having a nightcap. Slightly surprised, but very friendly, they informed us that in Bruinisse there is no Immigration or Customs office, we were too far inland. One telephone call took care of all formalities. We were impressed.

After a restful night, we were awakened in the morning by greetings in Polish. Even on such a small island, less then twenty miles long, there was a Pole. He was asked to keep *Chatka* from departing until the newspaper men arrive, already on their way from Antwerp, less then forty miles away. It was not exactly what we had in mind; at that time the tidal current was flowing in the desired direction. We left at one o'clock in the afternoon, taking the route by East Schelde, part of a great delta, leaving Schouwen Island on our starboard. We learned the reason for scarcity of harbors on that island: most of it consists of reclaimed land, it lies in a depression, below sea level. Only an area around Bruinisse and a sliver of the western part of Schouwen is on land not prone to floods.[10] When finally under

---

[10] Not anymore. The great project "Delta" put a series of mighty dams between mainland Holland, Goeree Island, Schouwen Island, North Beveland Island, and when it finally reached Zeeland, an enormous delta was enclosed. This work was designed to put an end to floods during the "storm surge" when high tides (which occur near the time of a full or new moon) coincide with the storm blowing towards the shore.

way, the weather for a change was cooperating; a NW, and later a NE wind pushed us swiftly towards Ostend, our next planned port, where we hoped to get some mail.

It was easy sailing in protected waters with a fair wind and a favorable current. Then the current changed, as expected, for the contrary, the wind was becoming weaker and weaker, and at the entrance to the harbor of Ostend we were practically stationary, rocking on the swell that was pushing us towards the western breakwater—a nasty structure with its wooden lining broken and in disarray. But old rusty bolts, once holding wood in place, now projecting for many inches, were still there. We had to use oars, just for the last hundred yards or so. No problem.

While under oars, out of nowhere came a deluge, in a matter of seconds we were thoroughly wet. We were totally unprepared for this kind of situation, the weather had been mild, the sky clear, and we had not taken any standard precautions; the freak rain did not last more than ten minutes, already in clear weather, around sunrise, *Chatka* was moored to the pontoon of the North Sea Yacht Club. We were very tired but we decided that it was not wise to go to sleep in soaked clothing, so we spread all the wet clothing, blankets, etc. for drying and took a stroll. The Post Office was still closed; we had to wait and continued our walk. Nearby was a commercial fishing harbor, the fishermen were unloading their catch. We had heard that a new specie of crab was brought accidentally to Europe from Asia and was making its way to the east towards Germany. It never occurred to us that this crab had already an important commercial significance for the fishermen of Belgium. Its common name was "woolly handed crab," for his pincers and legs were covered with a heavy growth of hair. The crab was big, more then two pounds, and very much in demand. Numbers of people were buying it right off the boat, for the equivalent of a few dollars apiece.

Finally it was time for the Post Office to open, we got a nice package of letters, our clothes had dried, and we returned to the boat. When we left *Chatka,* the tide started to flood, but was still low, now it had risen considerably, and all our drying was prominently exposed in a chic waterfront location. On the yard of yacht club flagpole the Polish flag was flying—a sign that a Polish boat was visiting, next to the boat was the usual gaggle of newspapermen. Order was made in a hurry, and I have to admit that the Belgians were very nice about our gaffe. In the evening, in the neat tent made with our sails, there was a small reception. Next morning, with a light land breeze we left that hospitable town—destination nearby Dunkirk, about 20 nautical miles of sailing. The winds were light and variable, it took a little longer than we had expected, but at the beginning of darkness we were in the entrance between breakwaters, western of solid construction and eastern made of a steel framework. Those piers extending far into the sea, were fairly well protecting the entrance channel from sizeable waves. The lattice of the eastern pier allowed the water of the coastal current to flow through, then directed it by the curved western structure to flow out to the sea. This arrangement was supposed to prevent shoaling of the entrance. Once more we were there near low water, the wind was blocked by the structures, the tide was pushing us against the breakwater's latticework which was well festooned by seaweed domesticated by all kinds of sea creatures. It was really fascinating, but instead of using the oars, like we did in Ostend, we had to push the boat along.

Progress was very slow, but the tide was going down rapidly, the concrete base of the pier became exposed, and it was possible to walk on that base and tow the boat. It was not easy, the concrete was in bad shape—there were gaps, holes—it was slippery. We reached the place where the lattice work was destroyed and was bridged by a makeshift suspended bridge. I could climb up on the twisted steel members, about 30 feet, until I got to the crown of the pier. I had a tow line with me; Janusz attached it to the mast and I could tow the boat faster, then there was an area of the big dip nets attached to the sizeable masts, those were in use only close to the high tide, but again it was a lot of work to carry the tow line around these contraptions. There was only one pleasant moment: when we were working to pass one of those big nets, a ship was entering the harbor. It was *m/s Fryderyk Chopin,* the Polish ship which we had hoped to meet at Dunkirk. At last we reached the land side ends of the piers, our sails got some wind, and soon *Chatka* moored at the Yacht Club de la Mer du Nord; it was four in the morning.

By sunrise, like in Ostend, a short heavy rain started falling. This time there was no problem, we were well sheltered. Dunkirk was our "alternate" port, some of the mail was supposed to be addressed there. Soon we learned that landing there was a big mistake.

The Yacht Club in Dunkirk is located in the midst of a commercial harbor, and in the morning all around were silhouettes of merchant ships, among them *Fryderyk Chopin*. It seemed to be very close, but Dunkirk harbor is a maze of basins, canals, different kinds of locks. It took us more than an hour to reach *Chopin*. Over there great and pleasant surprise: there were a number of alumni from the Maritime Academy, among them five colleagues from the same year, namely the electrician, the machinist, the radio officer, the assistant, and a sailor. With the last three we had spent years studying in the same room, Sparks left us only during the fourth year of study when he "deserted" to the Radio Department. The fact that an alumnus of the Navigation Department was employed as a sailor had shown the sad state of the Polish Merchant Marine. To wait for an officer's position could take a long time, so that in order to earn a living at sea one had to compromise. Soon the situation became so bad, that the Ministry of Maritime Affairs began to "lend" Polish marine officers to the fleets of developing countries, charging them a considerable part of their salary for the privilege.

In Poland, the profession of a merchant marine officer was a very coveted position. At the time when I had applied for admission, there were more than three thousand candidates for three hundred spots in the Navigation Department, the numbers were quite similar for aspiring naval mechanics. It was a great increase in numbers; years before classes had numbered about fifty. Moscow had decided that Poland would have a big merchant fleet serving the entire communist block. After finishing the first year, "navigators" were moved to the new school in Szczecin, close to the border with what was then East Germany. The new school's director was the Polish legend, Captain Konstanty Maciejewicz, a great sailor, pedagogue, and for many years the captain of *Dar Pomorza*. During the next year the Kremlin decided that a big Polish merchant fleet was not a great idea, and before we began our four-month tour on *Dar Pomorza* after second grade, our class numbered about fifty. On departure from Szczecin to Gdynia, where the square-rigger was stationed, Captain Maciejewicz organized an official send-off. Standing at attention we were ready for inspection. Communist official in charge of our group introduced me as the one at the head of the class "but an individualist," opinion rendered with disdain. I could see that Captain Maciejewicz did not understand why an official was disgusted; being of the old school the captain did not (yet) know that "individual-ist" in the communist parlance had become an invective.

On our return from the sea, we did not go back to Szczecin, but to the scaled-down school in Gdynia. The only attribute of the school's director there was the fact that he was a good communist (I am writing this with disdain). The previously tight connections of the alumni and school had deteriorated, but had not affected relations between individual graduates, every meeting among them, wherever it was, at any port of the seven seas became a small celebration. It was the same in Dunkirk.

Five of us had decided to look around town. It was impressive, and most entertaining when cars full of armed-to-the-teeth policemen came in droves, surrounded a block of the city, tumbling off and arresting anyone looking Algerian. Our Seamen's Books were supposed to be stamped in the police station. Big sign "DANGER" on the front of it was intimidating, but we were proceeding. Inside were cages, and in the cages were Algerians shouting insults at the police officers, who shouted insults back to the Algerians. It was quite a colorful scene. None of the policemen spoke any language except French, and in all the confusion they could not understand the reason for our visit. Fortunately one of the prisoners could speak some Spanish, I could too, so he translated our case into French and everything was settled amiably.

Next day we took a train to Bruay de Artois, about fifty miles south from Dunkirk, not far from Bethune, to visit a family of the Chief Officer from *Pilica,* the boat we had met in Goteborg. By chance, the Polish folk ensemble *Wesoly Tulacz*[11] was in town and celebrating their thirty-fifth anniversary on that day.

---

[11] "Happy homeless wanderer."

There was a custom, that when any of the group participating in the celebration was entering the stage, complete with their flags and banners, the head of the hosting club welcomed every one. We were honored to be included in the group representing the local Polish cell of the French Resistance, the famous Maquis. To our surprise and pleasure *Wesoly Tulacz* was not one of the-run-of-the mill bunch of amateurs. It was a really high-class musical ensemble. After a delightful evening we were surprised again, a representative of *Wesoly Tulacz* presented us with eight thousand francs, about a quarter of the sum we were allowed to take from Poland. Regretfully, we had to refuse sincere invitations to stay for the rest of a celebration; the meteorological forecast was favorable, strong easterly wind was expected. A fast train took us from Bethune to Dunkirk in less than an hour. Next morning, the forecast changed; easterly wind was to shift into a south western gale. Long-term prognosis was a strong northern. That was OK with us. We had not yet had the chance to try the boat in the stormy conditions on the close hauled course. After Bay of Biscayne such conditions would not be common, so we have decided to take this opportunity. Therefore when the tidal current changed for westerly, we were again at sea.

The favorable wind did not last long, when Calais was on our port beams, unpleasant southwestern was on again, blowing near gale, Force 7. While near the French shore it was easy to establish that *Chatka* was working against a strong drift current, about two knots. Never have I noticed such a strong drift current in this area during any of the passages I had done on the other vessels. Obviously there must have been a huge storm at the western end of the English Channel pushing in a great quantity of water. At night we could see the lightship *North Goodwin,* and on the port beams the lighthouse South Foreland. The tidal current was changing towards the shore, and we did not like the idea of sailing in this kind of weather in the vicinity of Goodwin Sands; those shoals can dry at low tide to show up ten feet so we decided to tack toward the south. At sunrise land was faintly visible almost directly on the course. Soon we identified it as Calais. The wind slackened a little, and we could carry a full suit of sails. Not long after the wind changed again and became southerly, again we were pushed back towards the North Sea. It was better to go west-northwest than south, so we tacked again. At about 2 PM in poor visibility, we saw a lightship, we had expected it to be the *East Goodwin,* but after approaching close enough to read its name we were not happy at all—it was *North Goodwin.* Not far away was port Ramsgate, near the northern tip of the peninsula separating Goodwin Sands from the Thames River. The tidal current was westerly, we had a good chance to enter the harbor. First tack did not bring us there, neither the second, and when we tacked again the tidal current had changed to the east. At that time *Chatka* was two miles from the Ramsgate entrance, two cables from the shore. Too bad.

There was no reason to keep sailing further north, we tacked again and sailed more or less south, depending on the shifting wind. The night was very dark, the moon was behind the low clouds. The weather was atrocious, squalls accompanied by heavy rain were drenching the boat and short, nasty, breaking waves were sending torrents of water over the boat, over her masts. It was not always possible to "take" the wave in a proper manner—a trick we had perfected during our trip on *Puchatek;* this would have required the wave to break against the windward bows and this did not always happen. Sometime a single, nasty, wave poured a few or even more than ten buckets of water into the boat. Salt water was irritating our eyes, lifting our eyelids was a painful process; then it was necessary to wait a few seconds in order to see something. Fortunately the water was not very cold.

Worst of all were the processions of ships; once, during a single hour we were passed by eight ships, one encounter every seven or eight minutes. Our running lights were weak, we were shining light on the sails, sometimes a ship would turn in the last moment, sometimes we had to head into the wind in order to let the ship pass some fifty feet in front of us. One encounter was really scary, it was at four in the morning, the time when watches are changing and vigilance on the bridge can be impaired. A small freighter, maybe two thousands tons, for sure big enough to smash *Chatka* into kindling, was on a collision course. All our lights did not produce any results. Finally we had to resort to the action we had dubbed "singe the lookout's mustache"—that is, fire a white rocket into the bridge. The ship did not turn at once, it took them a good time to change course, we did whatever we could, and collision was avoided, but barely. All this happened during a strong squall when our boat was "in chains" and the sails were in danger to be shredded, but everything ended fine.

During such a bad night none of us could go to sleep. When bailing out the boat we were counting the number of buckets; I emptied two tons of water, later Janusz another three tons. When morning came, we rested in relays, each catching a few hours of sleep. About noontime I spotted a town, soon it was obvious that it was Dunkirk. After shaking out two reefs from the storm mainsail, *Chatka* was moving faster, higher into the wind, the spray was heavier, but it did not matter. As usual, the most dramatic moment was at the entrance to the harbor. The lighthouse on the tip of the western pier took our wind, current was moving the boat toward the eastern structure, but soon the wind was again in our sails, and without any further problems we sailed to exactly the same spot which we had left three days before. It was practically the end of sailing season in northern France. We were given a free run of yacht club facilities, a small café where we could cook, couches where we could sleep, showers, to sum up in one word—luxury.

Outside a strong storm was blowing. The weather was sunny, our sails, blankets, and clothes were rinsed in fresh water and dried. We were very unhappy; we were stuck in Dunkirk for three days. Three days were not important, the important thing was that we were missing the strong wind from the north. The entrance to Dunkirk harbor was a melee of braking water and foam. It was impassable even for larger ships, to say nothing of the impossibility of tacking a lifeboat against the storm in the narrow entrance channel built perpendicular to the shore, almost in a north-south direction. Had we not called on Dunkirk at all, had we gone some twenty miles farther, had we stopped in Dover, waited out the southwester there, we could have left at the beginning of the northern, and instead of sitting in the hospitable Yacht Club de la Mer du Nord, we would have had the English Channel behind us, and would be sailing the open Atlantic.

6

*Straits of Dover—Dover—Waiting for the change
of weather—Trip to London—Bad storm—Unusual
entrance to Boulogne.*

T HREE DAYS LATTER the storm has blown itself out, with
the light north-northeast *Chatka* left the port of Dunkirk,
and again we were going towards the Straits of Dover. It was
obvious that the favorable wind, a leftover from the high
pressure system, would soon yield to another "low" with its
southwestern. That happened soon enough, when we were
entering the roadstead of Dover—a huge area enclosed by
miles of breakwaters—the wind changed to southwest. To
enter the docks of Dover is not a simple and easy matter. The
locks at the entrance to the docks are open only for a short
time near high water—*Chatka* was lying at her anchor for
more than ten hours, finally, late at night we passed the lock
and entered Wellington Dock. I informed the dock master that
we shall be leaving very soon, in two or three days, when the
anticipated change of weather would come, and I asked him
for a berth near the entrance. He placed us alongside a big
ketch with a broken bowsprit. Her crew, apparently a family,
was working hard repairing the damage. Whenever leaving
the boat, we had to pass through their deck, they were very
nice about it, cheerfully answering our greetings, but I never
noticed an instant of their talking to each other.

The anticipated change of weather did not come for a long
time. Wellington Dock was getting crowded with yachts com-

ing south from the eastern coast of England with the intention of moving west to the ports of the Channel or trying to get to the Atlantic. Boats were moored alongside in two rows, then three, then four. *Chatka* was no longer in a place from which it would be easy to reach the entrance to the lock, she was separated by two rows of waiting boats. *Venture,* a big ketch of classical lines, was moored nearby. Her skipper, Bob Curtis, became our friend; together we spent a lot of time in the local yacht club, watching frequent weather forecasts on TV. Whenever a low pressure system started to occlude, with forced optimism we assured each other that "tomorrow we are leaving." After a short walk to visit the dock master we informed him that "if there was no sudden change in the weather forecast, we would be leaving with the next high water." Invariably, the next broadcast of the synoptic map was showing the next low pressure system creeping from the west. It was a very bad year for any sailing vessel trying to proceed west, such a constant procession of southwesters would have been expected a few weeks later in the season.

Frustrated, when there was no longer any hope of change of weather in the next few days; we decided to make a short trip to London. A hitchhiked pickup took us "nearest to the City," then we took a bus, asked to be told when we shall be "nearest to the City," we were told to stay on the bus to the end of its line. Then we took a train (to its last station), finally the subway took us to the center of London. We had not realized that this short trip (about fifty miles) would take such a long time, it was already well after dark, and it was raining. We found a Polish Club, where we were invited to spend the night. The next day was less adventurous. We visited the Association of Polish Merchant Navy Officers in London, a most pleasant visit, and we spent a few hours conversing with our older colleagues, the Maritime Academy alumni. We were eager to hear their wartime stories, how they had coped in the foreign merchant navies; they were interested in how the situation had shaped in Poland under the communist rule.

It would have been a real faux pas to be in London and not to visit the British Museum. We visited it, our only regret being that we could not spend there days instead of hours.

As well we secured a most important gadget: a battery powered radio (ours had gone bad just after a few days of sailing). Our previous navigation was relatively easy; in confined realms of the Baltic Sea, Kattegat, Skagerrak, the North Sea we did not have much use for astronavigation, besides, we could have checked our watches, knowing our exact position from terrestrial sights and working "in reverse" to calculate the exact time. During the forthcoming ocean navigation that would be impossible, but a radio would give us the possibility to receive time signals. The Company RCA-Radio gave us such a receiver, it had a directional antenna and we could use it to take approximate bearings for radio stations. Back to Dover. Back to waiting for a change of weather.

During the following days rain was followed by drizzle, drizzle by rain. Coal dust was blown from the shore, all the yachts in Wellington Dock were covered with a black slurry. The temperature was lower and lower, our spirits were sagging. Finally we could not stand it anymore. After twelve days of waiting, when the forecast was not as bad as usual (variable winds from western directions, Force 5 or less), we left the dock at high water, dropped anchor in the sheltered roadstead, and waited for a favorable tidal current to help us sail outside the breakwaters. This plan did not work well; at dawn the wind freshened and the anchor began to drag, we were pushed in the corner between the boulevard and the oil terminal breakwater. We had to tack with our course straight against the wind, then near the entrance, the wind veered just when the boat was coming about, and *Chatka* was very near the breakwater. Fortunately the waves were small, we could have fought out that predicament, but a friendly crew of a small tugboat which was passing by gave us a tow into the Channel.

Our previously gained experience, when we had so many problems between Ramsgate and Dunkirk, taught us an important lesson: even if sailing is hard, try to manage the boat single-handed, giving the second of the crew the possibility to rest. The idea of keeping away from the shipping lanes was obvious, only this time we had more sea room and we could do it. The wind was constantly changing towards the south, and with the first tack we did not manage to gain much, the second tack was practically parallel to the shore, and we reached the vicinity of Dieppe. That was something. There was a lot of working with the sails, the wind was changing between the south and the southwest; when south, we were sailing on the port tack, when southwest, on the starboard tack. As we learned later, we were passed by three low pressure systems.

In order to keep rested as much as possible, we were working six-hour on, six-hour off. During one such watch Janusz had to tack eight times. Force 5 wind became Force 6, then Force 7, then suddenly increased to Force 10. Seas were high again, about 25 feet, breaking heavily. During that storm we did not have much chance to make headway, all our energy was spent on not losing what we had gained. This strategy paid off: after three and a half days, while approaching the English shore, the *Royal Sovereign*—the lightship anchored not far from Beachy Head—was on *Chatka* bows. The storm has eased off, the welcomed Force 6 was with us again. During a pleasant sundown we were both at the stern sheets, engaged in pleasant conversation. Suddenly, out of nowhere, an enormous comber rose above our boat and we were swamped. I was steering, positioned on the windward side, and I had some protection of the gunwale. Janusz was on the lee side of the boat. When I saw Janusz being lifted by the water and rising above the lee gunwale, I let go of the tiller, grabbed him by his oilskin pants, at the same time holding the windward gunwale with my right hand. In that way we both stayed in the boat, which was almost full of water. The unattended rudder was lifted out of its hinges and trailed behind the boat, secured by a line, fixed exactly for such an occasion.

First we dropped the main, then hinged the rudder. For a while we considered using the steering oar, but the seas calmed considerably; hinging the rudder took, I think, less than a minute. Our steering compass was gone. It had been fixed with good size screws to the stern platform.

With only a small jib (about 5 square feet) we turned the boat with the wind, and began to bail out the water. We worked as fast as we could, taking turns every hundred buckets. The lack of steering compass did not bother us much, we were simply trying to keep the boat with the wind. After about an hour and a half, when the water level went below two feet, a pleasant discovery: the steering compass was in the boat! Another hour

Janusz at the mainmast, checking the rigging.

and the boat was "dry." We were tired, but it did not matter much, our problem was the cold. It was already the thirteenth of October. Again, everything was thoroughly wet, and with the weather we could expect for another week or two, drying of the blankets, clothes, etc. was out of the question. Visibility was good, and we decided to go to Boulogne-sur-Mer. We did not have much of a choice, but at least we still would be in the English Channel. Navigation was easy, the wind was slackening rapidly, we could carry more canvas and we shook out the reefs. We thought we knew where we were, namely, quite near the entrance to the port of Boulogne, but we could not see the lights marking the heads of the breakwater. I took new bearings for the nearby lighthouses. I took those bearings VERY carefully. VERY carefully I plotted the position. I was flabbergasted.

"According to that crazy position we are exactly in the entrance!"

"Look there!" Janusz answered pointing toward something on our starboard, high in the air. The very high wall of the breakwater with a tall, solid light tower was slowly moving astern. It was near low water, nevertheless the tidal current was still flowing out of the harbor, and in the light wind *Chatka* was barely making headway, but we were in Boulogne-sur-Mer. Not knowing where to look for a yacht club (it was not a good time to pay somebody a visit anyway, it was close to one o'clock in the morning), we moored alongside a tugboat which we spotted at a nearby quay. She was a steamer and her boilers were on, keeping the pressure. We were so cold that we were shivering. Our French was atrocious, but it was obvious to the mechanic on duty that we were very cold, and he kindly let us into the engine room. We took a few wet blankets and positioned ourselves in the warmest part, on the grid just below the roof of the engine room. We fell asleep in seconds, still shivering. After a few hours we awoke parched, our throats dry, our blankets stiff with dried salt. Looking for the warmest place, we did not realize that we slightly overdid it, on our perch the temperature was about 105 degrees Fahrenheit. A few glasses of water restored our ability to speak. Sunrise was approaching and the tugboat was making ready for its workday. The skipper spoke English, and our first question was about the entrance lights, why were they not lit? If the wind were stronger it was very easy to get smashed against the

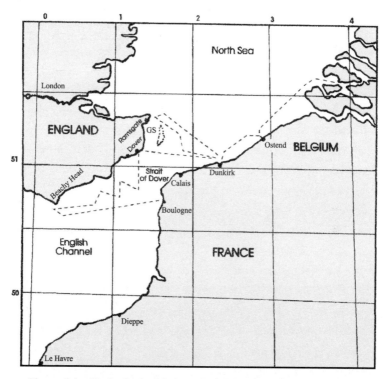

Chart of the Chatka Puchatków's *course from the Bruinisse in Holland, to Ostend in Belgium, and Dunkirk in France. Stormy, unsuccessful trial to pass the Dover Strait, followed by the passage to Dover, and finally, to Boulogne in France. Short single-handed trip close to the coast, from Boulogne to Calais is not shown. On this chart the Goodwin Sands are marked by "GS."*

breakwater. His answer was shocking: "Nobody is expected to enter during the time of low water. They were off as an economy measure." Assuming that lights were 500 watts units, and were shut off for 6 hours around the low water, then savings would be 3 kWh, about 30 cents per day per light!

The skipper showed us the location of the yacht club; we sailed there leisurely and, as usual, we were given all the courtesy, comfortable mooring and the use of the clubhouse. We were shown the morning newspaper. It was full of stories about yesterday's storm. About the unexpected and sudden rise in power that exceeded Force 10, about the number of distress signals SOS, the destruction it left in the port of Dunkirk, etc., etc. We felt that after all, we did not do all that badly.

7

What to do?—Paris—Dr. Bombard—Solitary trip to Calais—Hyperion—The first canals—Outboard engine—Leaving Bethune

*W*E HAD TO FACE THE FACT: it was too cold to continue our trials to force the English Channel the way we were doing. Without any shadow of doubt we had proved that the lifeboat can be sailed in the most difficult conditions and that we know how to do it. If we tried once more, most likely we would again have gained some ground, but it would prove nothing more but our resistance to the cold weather and salt water.

After considering all our options we had to disregard the easiest one: to wait until next spring. There were many reasons against it; our canned food supply for about eight weeks was considered "untouchable," it was to be used at sea. If we were to wait in France we would have to find some means of supporting ourselves. That we could do, but to get a "work permit" could prove time consuming and frustrating. We could "catch a ride" on any Polish ship and winter in Poland, but in that case *Chatka* would have to be abandoned for many months, all the equipment and supply would be in jeopardy, to say nothing of the wintry deterioration of the boat herself. Also, there was the problem with the communist bureaucracy in Poland, the prospect of securing all the permits anew was hair-raising. Of one thing we were certain, there would be a few "friends" who would declare our expedition a failure.

There was another possibility: to equip our boat with an outboard motor which would allow us to enter small harbors, and using favorable tidal currents to go west in six hourly "hops" until we reached Brest, or even cabotage farther south to Spain and warmer weather. The third version was again to get an engine and go through French canals and rivers down to Marseille and the Mediterranean.

From the backwaters of Boulogne-sur-Mer to the city of lights, Paris, it is only about 120 miles. Hitchhiking did not go well. We arrived in the outskirts of the capital of France late in the evening, there was not a hotel in sight, we walked and walked in the direction of the center. Streets were empty of people and traffic. Soon it became apparent that the same car was passing us, turning right on the next corner, then reappearing driving slowly behind us and repeating the maneuver at the end of another city block. After repeating this five or six times, suddenly the car jumped onto the curb, all four doors flew open, and we were surrounded by five men armed with automatic guns, similar to the Kalashnikovs, well known to us. It did not take long to understand that we were taken for Algerians on the way to mischief. Handing them our "seamen's books" cleared the atmosphere; we asked for and were given directions to the nearby tiny hotel.

The next day was very different, nearby was the terminal of Metro, we boarded the train and in a short time we were in the Latin Quarter, there was a student's club of which I was aware.[12] All the attention given us in northern France had an

---

[12] While I was waiting for Janusz, whose ship arrived in Gdynia a few months after my *Piast,* I started to study the physics. Before we sailed on *Chatka Puchatków* I secured an official break in studies, therefore I could be considered a student.

echo in most newspapers and magazines in Paris, including *Paris Match*. Suddenly we were the center of attention, it seemed that all doors were open for us. We were invited to meet Dr. Allen Bombard, an acknowledged expert on survival at sea. His previous research and our goals were similar: find how to maximize the chance for survival on a small boat in a situation when the ship has to be abandoned. Our meeting went very well, and we immediately received two offers: one from Dr. Bombard himself, to join his expedition in the Canary Islands. It was supposed to be in progress until April next year, its end would wonderfully coincide with good sailing weather in northern Europe. Unfortunately, in that case *Chatka Puchatków* would have to spend the winter in Boulogne-sur-Mer. The second offer was from the publishing company *Edition Paris,* the same company which published Bombard's book about his crossing the Atlantic in a rubber raft. The offer was tempting, the first 100,000 francs was to be paid immediately, as a payment securing their right to our story.

Just then, when everything was going in our favor, one of Bombard's experiments went bad: during the stormy weather in the Bay of Biscay a group of people during the simulated shipwreck, was trying to cross the surf and land on the sandy beach. A number of the participants were drowned. Suddenly, from one day to the next, from being a national hero, Bombard was accused of reckless behavior and senseless experiments. The French press had a heyday; lifesaving experts were multiplying at breakneck pace. Every freshly baked expert knew exactly what went wrong; everyone had a different opinion. Time was flying; *Edition Paris* was not so sure about commercial success of our (future) book. We realized that the cost of an engine strong enough to be useful at sea was higher than we could afford, even with those 100,000 francs. We decided to try the canal and river routes to Marseille.

Boulogne is not part of the French inland waterway system; *Chatka* had to be moved to Calais. The weather forecast was favorable: light winds from westerly directions. There were still some unfinished business affairs to be attended to in Paris, so it was decided that Janusz would stay in Paris and I would travel to Boulogne-sur-Mer and single-handed sail to Calais, a distance of only about twenty-five miles. Winds were light, so light that they were practically nonexistent, but I managed to exit Boulogne-sur-Mer, then with a gentle breeze I followed the coast more or less north, past Cape Gris-Nez, then changed course for more easterly. Evening came, wind slackened even more, a contrary tidal current was mowing faster than *Chatka* under sail, and I started to move back to Cape Gris-Nez. The water was shallow, the sea calm, I dropped the anchor, then dropped the sails. It was bitterly cold, I was dozing off, not daring to go to sleep. I hoisted the anchor light, but no ships were coming so close to the shore, there were no small fishing boats at night. Morning came and with the morning came the fog. Initially I could not see the sun at all. Then it was a glare, soon after I could see a diffused disc. Finally the sun won, only here and there wisps of fog were left, nearby land became visible. Also, the tidal current changed, and I could hoist the anchor and slowly sail towards Calais. Near the entrance to the harbor the wind almost died, but the sun operated strongly and I hoped for a sea breeze. Likewise with radiation fog from the previous night, it was easy to predict that when the air warmed up, the fog would disperse, same with the sea breeze, it was easy to predict that around noontime it would start blowing. Unfortunately prediction of weather is a risky business. Still becalmed so near my destination, I was looking towards the sea, hoping to see some ripples on the water heralding the approaching wind. Finally, it came! Slowly but surely *Chatka*

Puchatków entered the harbor, and I moored her at the entrance to the Canal de Calais.

Happy with myself, but still frozen stiff, I decided to celebrate my solitary sail by checking into a small hotel, where I had a hot meal, a bottle of white Bordeaux and a comfortable bed. That treat set me back $1.25.

The next morning, well refreshed, I started to prepare the boat for inland travel. I unstepped both masts, using the sails I made a more permanent tent on the stern, I gave the boat a real good cleaning, improvised a tiny mast on which the Polish flag could be hoisted. On its masthead the little pennant of the expedition was attached: the same golden teddy bear on the green background, as the one we had used during trip of *Puchatek*. Before the end of the day, the motor yacht *Hyperion* moored near me. She was crewed by two employees of the Yacht Transport, a British company specializing in sailing any kind of pleasure craft whenever the owner did not want, or could not do it personally, but wanted to have a boat at a certain place. The owner of *Hyperion* wanted to have her in Monte Carlo, and Yacht Transport was delivering her there.

I was to meet Janusz in Bethune, about fifty miles from Calais. My idea was to hitch a ride with a barge. When I walked to the lock separating the fresh water canal from the salt water of port of Calais, I found that it would be a problem—sizes of locks were standardized, therefore barges, for economical reasons, were built to fit the lock exactly. So exactly that after the barge entered the lock, her rudder had to be put at an angle of 90 degrees. That was necessary because otherwise the lock's gate would not be able to close behind the barge. For sure, there was no room for both barge and *Chatka* in the lock. I was considering pulling my boat in and out of the lock, but that could be cumbersome. The appearance of the *Hyperion* was heaven-sent; she was bigger then *Chatka,* but both boats could fit in the lock very comfortably. I asked the skipper if he could give me a tow to Bethune and he agreed immediately. Some formalities had to be taken care of, but it seemed that everyone was aware of *Chatka* and I was presented with a number of official papers, which supposedly were sufficient for us to cross France legally.

When it was time for dinner, the British crew of *Hyperion* invited me to join them on their boat. I dug out the best Polish canned ham we had on the boat—it was appreciated onboard of *Hyperion*. While in England, we never knew that British newspapers were writing anything about our trip. When in France, we were met with "admiration," which was quite embarrassing; in England, it seemed to us nobody was really interested in our adventures. People were friendly and helpful; we simply assumed that seafaring people were reacting with understanding to the problems of other sailors. It was not so; Peter, the skipper of *Hyperion* on her trip from England to Monte Carlo, knew about us, read about our departure from Dover, and was worrying about us when the big unexpected storm hit the English Channel. I told him that he was right, we did have some difficult times—for example when the big breaking wave almost took Janusz overboard. After hearing this narrative he presented me with two high-quality safety harnesses, saying, "So in the future you will not have to hold each other by the pants."

Peter was just a few years older than I, but he managed to accumulate vast sailing experience. During the very pleasant evening, he told us about some sailing trips in unfriendly regions during times of dangerous weather. The most adventurous trip he considered to be was the delivering of a small coastal motor yacht from Bermuda to England. Another temporary crew member of *Hyperion* was older than both Peter and I. During the Second World War the Germans took him prisoner of war, and he was held in the camp located in occupied Poland. He was very fond of the Polish population who were trying to help the allied POWs, an activity that carried the risk of being shot on the spot. He even learned some Polish words: dziękuję, dzień dobry, chleba (thank you, good morning, bread).[13]

The departure date was 31st of October. Peter did not plan to sail far, we wanted to pass the first lock and start the next day early in the morning. For a reason totally unknown to me, the hunchbacked guardian of the lock felt great antipathy for *Chatka Puchatków* and her one-person crew. My contact with him was limited to handing him a sheaf of papers issued by Harbor Master and Custom offices, I did not speak to him, for the simple reason that at that time my French vocabulary consisted of but a few words. According to him, the documents were lacking some signature. The crew of the *Hyperion* was trying to convince him that *Chatka* is without an engine and that signature is not necessary. His answer was that soon he would close the lock, because five o'clock is approaching. I had to run fifteen minutes sprint to the Harbor Master's office, get an extra signature, and run back. Peter was fussing in the lock until I, short of breath, was back, he exited the lock again, took my towline, and together we had moored in front of the tiny office of my tormentor. He did not like the idea that I would be out of his grab, he was scrutinizing my papers, looking for some other omissions. I heard a beautifully put together bunch of English oaths, courtesy of Peter. It was

---

[13] Not an exact translation. The expression "good morning" is not used in Polish, before late afternoon it is always "good day." Exact translation of "bread" is "chleb," but in Polish nouns are defined (up to seven ways), "chleba" means "I need (want) bread." Other variations of the noun bread: chlebowi, chlebem, chlebie.

impressive even to the ear of a Merchant Mariner. Another Frenchman, a superior of the hunchback, took the papers, had one look at them and let us into the lock.

The next night I spent in the company of the British again, and early Sunday morning we were under way. The sun was bright and the northerly wind was hardly noticeable, it was a fine fall day, the last warm day of the year, as I found out later. That day we arrived at Les Fontinettes and took our place in the queue of barges waiting to be lifted to the higher level by an enormous hydraulic crane. Imagine four canals running parallel to each other, two on the ground level, another two at the height of a four story building,[14] sitting on a steel trestle structure. The last hundred feet or so of one of the lower canals and one of the upper canals are in the form of vast steel tubs. Between those tubs and the rest of the canals there are four pairs of vertically moving doors. If all doors are up, the tubs and the ends of canals are sealed. Then the tubs are lifted (lower one), or lowered (upper).

The procedure is as follows: barges (very carefully!) enter both the lower and the upper tub. The doors are raised, sealing both canals and tubs. Hydraulic machinery rises one tub and lowers the other, to the position that both tubs are next to the canals, then two doors (one sealing the tub and one sealing the end of the canal) at the front of each barge are lowered, then each barge proceeds forward, each on a different level.

If the barges are of different weight, or if in one tub is a barge and in another *Chatka Puchatków* it does not matter, the weight of the water in the tub plus boats would be the same. Archimedes sends his regards: a craft or crafts entering the tub will replace exactly the amount of water weighing as much as the weight of the boats in the tub.

---

[14] Exactly 13.13 meters (43 feet).

The whole machinery was built in the 1880s, during the Industrial Revolution, as a replacement of a series of five locks built about hundred years earlier, still in existence, but rarely used. It makes a great impression, big quantity of levers, counterweights, cranks, pistons, everything in motion, cascades of water sloshing out of tubs, enormity of scale. As I had mentioned it was Sunday and a nice, sunny day. Nearby observation platforms were full of visitors. On the side of canals whole families were picnicking. Obviously, even locals are still attracted by the spectacle. The spectacle was closed at 5:30 PM, we did not make it to the lift that day and had to spend a night on the lower level, the efficiency of the lift was not great.[15] During the evening conversation I learned that on the way to Marseille I would have to pass 225 locks (!), to say nothing of the more than a hundred low bridges, bascule, swinging, draw, and whatever other design French engineers had dreamt of in the nineteen century.

To Bethune there were only four locks, Monday morning we were lifted by the mechanical monstrosity; other locks were of standard type and we did not have to wait a long time to pass through. In the early afternoon we were in Bethune. I thanked Peter for the tow, we wished each other a good trip.

Bethune was almost a Polish city in the midst of France. Many signs were in Polish, French kids were in minority and most of them could speak Polish which they picked up from their playmates. In the cafes, the music boxes were playing Polish melodies.

---

[15] Nine years later the boat lift in Les Fontinettes was replaced by a single lock, but all the machinery, including ancient five step locks are preserved as a kind of an open air museum.

Our previous idea of hitchhiking by the barge, as I had explained before, was totally impractical, I had to find some kind of an engine. The Polish community in Bethune consisted mainly of miners, working numerous mines in the area. Boating was not their most common pastime. I could not find any old motor that could be fixed and then returned to the owner. The Polish newspapers sent a message about our plight, but there was no response.

I had two extra problems: according to our agreement with Janusz, he would meet me in the Yacht Club in Calais. Whenever I was not on the premises I would leave a message where I could be found. Our next point of communication was general delivery, Post Office Bethune. I did not have any message there either. The second problem was my French visa, it was about to expire. The nearest Polish Consulate was in Lille, some paltry fifteen miles away. I went there, expecting a standard, cold-shoulderish kind of reception, even though what I wanted was simply to be helped with the French visa.

Surprise, surprise, surprise, I was welcomed there. Our good friend, Staszek Mioduszewski, who was acting as our one man supporting office in Poland, had skillfully used all the positive publicity we had generated and persuaded the head of the Polish Ministry of Maritime Affairs to help us in our trip through France. I had met Minister Darski a few times before, during the planning stage of the expedition, and have found him quite sympathetic to our goals.

Consul Zamiara in Lille had a letter from the ministry to that effect, besides that, there were 55,000 francs waiting for us, courtesy of the same ministry. In such an unexpected and simple way our biggest problems disappeared. Our emergency contact with Janusz was a telephone call at the students club in Paris. Immediately I called the club and left a message for Janusz, setting the next day for a meeting at the Polish Consulate in Paris.

By a lucky coincidence, the Polish consul in Lille had to be in Paris the next day as well for a conference. After a comfortable night in Lille we drove to Paris, I met Janusz, and together we went shopping for an outboard engine—secondhand, of course. The selection was very good, but prices were bad, we had to settle for a nondescript motor, of uncertain power, something between three and five horsepower, with the plaque stating its birthday—it was exactly 21 years old, same as I. Also we bought maps of the French inland waterways. We were very happy.

The consul was scheduled to leave in the evening. The few hours of free time I spent saying good bye to the number of friends I made during the almost two-week period I had spent in Paris at my previous stay there, which of itself was an adventure. Penniless, we had to try to work wherever it was possible. My student's identity card was helpful, we could get some low paying jobs in the famous Parisian Halls, an enormous wholesale market supplying food for most of the French Capital, open during the night. At dawn, when the Hales were closing, one could fortify himself in one of the seemingly countless tiny restaurants in the vicinity, well known for their onion soup. Evenings in the student club, reading poetry of nonconformist Polish poet Ildefons Gałczyński. Lots of interviews with French newspapermen, then return again to the very bleak reality. All in all, I cannot say that I really liked Paris and it's way of life. On the other hand, a lot of my acquaintances were living in the tiny attic apartments of the dilapidated buildings, but it was the Latin Quarter and they acted or behaved quite happy of their lot. Even harassment from intrusive landladies did not seem to bother them much.

Returning in the evening in the well loaded car (four passengers, the driver plus the motor), we were delivered right to the *Chatka,* moored in the inland port of Bethune.

In that city there was a sizeable Polish boarding school run by Polish clergy. In its dormitory I found lodging during my previous stay in Bethune. It had a well-equipped workshop where we could make a fitting to adapt the engine to the boat. The engine was so small that it would be unpracticable to make a contraption to mount it to the gunwale; instead, we got the idea to attach it to the rudder. This had an additional advantage: *Chatka* would have an "active rudder": when the tiller was put in a 90-degree position, the boat could be turned around without any forward movement. That feature would help us a lot in the tight quarters often encountered during inland sailing. The president of one of the Polish societies, Mr. Borgus, was extremely helpful. He found a mechanic who knew a bit about ancient outboard motors and gave ours a good check.

Tiny engine mounted on the rudder.

We were "adopted" by the Polish Bethune. Locals showered us with kindness, invitations for dinners, gifts. I am afraid that sometimes we were not polite because we were forced to decline participation in some affairs. It was already November, soon the canals would be frozen and we wanted to move south towards the warmer weather. Working on the engine mount, checking the working of the contraption took more time than we had expected, but we did not want to leave this friendly town before we were sure that everything was in perfect order. The motor had two cylinders, both spark plugs were fouling in a matter of minutes. We, and the mechanic, could not find the reason.

One of the many kibitzes took one sniff of the gasoline and declared it a culprit. We bought new fuel, mixed it with oil and pronto: the motor was working like a charm.

There were other chores to do, but soon everything we could think of was done. The local housewives supplied us with a seemingly inexhaustible supply of fresh victuals, and we were ready to move on. The river port of Bethune consists of a dug out sizeable basin connected to the Canal de la Bassée by two short access canals; in that way the barge does not have to turn inside the basin, it can move forward and reach main canal south or north of the town. Not wanting to make

In Bethune, posing for a Polish newspaper.

a stir by our departure, we left the port after dark, moving toward the southern entrance. A short distance from the port the canal was blocked by a few barges moored along side each other. We tied the boat to the shore and boarded the raft of barges and, in a carefree mood, moved towards one that had some light showing through the bull-eyes of its cabin, trying to find the way around. At the sound of our boots on the iron deck, a man came outside, his face was strangely contorted, and he said something in a sad sounding voice. I did not understand. Looking away from us, he repeated the same words, this time practically shouting, his face illuminated by the light shining from the cabin below, which presented a really unearthly sight. I have to admit, I felt spooky. We were standing in silence, the Frenchman finally noticed that we did not understand what he was saying and pointed his hand towards the stern of the barge. Over there I could see the dark shape of a flag, it was at half-staff. I said "pardon," and pulled Janusz towards the shore. Soon he noticed the position of the flag and understood what it meant: on the barge there was a body of a bargeman, lying in state. We turned the *Chatka* around and reached the main canal by the northern entrance. Our mood had changed from carefree to uncomfortable. What a way to start our cross-France trip!

In a short time we reached the Canal de la Bassée, leading east towards the junction with the Canal de la Deude. After two hours of motoring, a little more then ten kilometers farther, we had to stop at the entrance to our first lock, at Cuinchy.

8

Problems with the French—Tunnels—Alone again—
Two solitary sailors—French canals—Problems with
the engine—Saone River—Sailing down the river—
Rhone River—Flood.

SEEMINGLY, THE TASK was not monumental; there were about one thousand kilometers from Calais to Marseilles. During the first day after Bethune we established our exact speed, it was six kilometers per hour. It seemed that in less than 200 hours of sailing we could do it. For sure we could be under way for twelve hours a day, in little over two weeks we could be on the Mediterranean, in the Gulf of Lions. But reality proved to be very different. French locks and draw-bridges could be opened only during eight hours a day, in some places they were closed for Sundays. Sometimes, in order to enter a different canal it was necessary to wait more than a day, a similar situation to the one I had encountered at Las Fontinettes, when we were leaving the canalized Aa River and entering Canal Neufosse. For the next few days it was easy—tolerable weather, locks spaced a few kilometers apart, light barge traffic—we were making good progress. Canal de la Deule was behind us, Canal de la Sensee, the Escaut River as well, and at Cambrai we reached Canal St. Quentin. During that time we were eating like kings; gourmet delicacies supplied by the housewives in Bethune lasted for a good while.

To make our suppers more enjoyable we were buying local wines at a standard price 25 cents a bottle. Knowing where there was a lock, which we would not be able to pass that

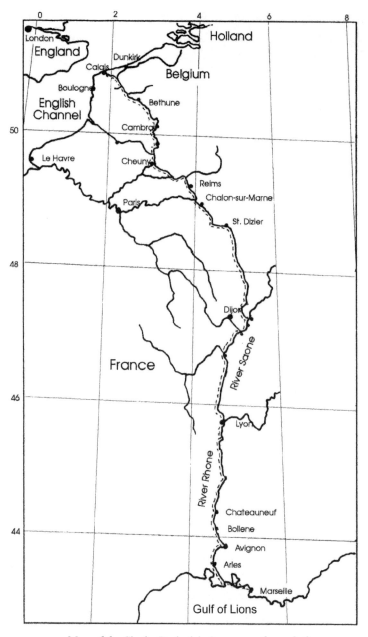

Map of the Chatka Puchatków's *voyage through the canals and rivers of France, from Calais to Marseille.*

afternoon because of the end of the working day, we would select a nice spot for the night. It could even be quite far from the lock, we could get up early and easily motor there before the workday started. We would stop at the nearby village store and, using our extremely limited French, ask for a bottle of wine. Trying to pronounce the French "vin" in a Polish, English, or German way did not produce any results. In order to be understood it was always necessary to point to the bottle of the desired wine. During one fine evening, while sitting at the small campfire on the bank of a canal, we were discussing this strange linguistic problem. Suddenly I remembered that I brought with me a small book in Polish on the basics of the French Language. In the morning I found that book in a watertight container, and it was soon obvious that "vin" is pronounced "vę" in Polish. The sound "ę" does not exist in English; some call it a "nasal e." When I told Janusz about my findings his answer was "Impossible." It was easy to check. The same evening, when I asked for ordinary "vin rouge" I was handed a one liter bottle of the local red wine. Janusz was amazed.

If not for the pressure of time, our trip could have been pleasant. A few kilometers from any village the canal banks were totally deserted. There was plenty of firewood, and we could do all our cooking on the shore; it was easier and more enjoyable than cooking on board using a kerosene stove.

The canals themselves were very interesting. Built in the nineteenth century, at different times, they differed in construction and the locks were of various designs.[16] Taking into account that most structures were more than 150 years old, it was difficult not to be impressed.

---

[16] Since our trip many canals from Calais to Bauvin (the entrance to the Canal de la Deude) were modernized. Some locks were enlarged, some difficult jointures were straightened out.

Canal St. Quentin is a good example. First, the southern part was open in 1738. From there it was stop and go, disputes about the final route, the necessity of constructing an expensive tunnel, wars with England, final construction postponed until 1801 when Napoleon ordered to move on with the works. Old plans, originally presented in 1727 were dug out, and the completed canal was opened in 1810. It is almost a hundred kilometers long, with 35 locks.

After 29 kilometers and 17 locks, on the ninth of November, we were at the entrance of a great tunnel, almost six kilometers long, which took its name from a nearby village, Bony. It was possible to pass it under our own power, or by being towed by an electric "mule." The official did not have much faith in our tiny motor and ordered us to wait for the end of the convoy.[17] This wait would take many hours. Fortunately the skipper of one of the barges graciously offered us a tow. For safety reasons the speed through this tunnel is set at 4 kilometers per hour; it took us about an hour and a half before we were again in daylight, it was already afternoon. We thanked him for the tow, and under our own power we motored about seven kilometers of a level canal leading to the second tunnel (named Tronquoy), in front of which another convoy was being formed. Having learned from our previous experience we asked the skipper of the first barge to tow us through. This tunnel was less than a kilometer and half long; in half an hour we were in front of the first downhill lock, towards the city of St. Quentin.

---

[17] Traffic on the summit level, about 20 kilometers long (including two tunnels) is one way. All the crafts proceeding in the same direction are marshaled into a convoy. When it passes, which takes the better part of the day, the convoy going in the opposite direction begins its trip the next morning.

Another fifty something kilometers, and it was the end of the Canal St. Quentin. In Chauny we entered, for a short distance, Canal Lateral a l'Oise in order to reach Canal de l'Oise a l'Aisne, connecting two rivers: Oise and Aisne.

The idea of a "canal lateral" or a "parallel canal" is an excellent one. Instead of canalizing a river and therefore destroying its beauty (if there is any) and its natural aspects, for example marshes providing habitat for wildlife, its course is less winding than the original river and a barge has a shorter distance to travel. There are some engineering problems. One of the most difficult to solve: how a canal can cross a river? It was solved in a very elegant manner: an aqueduct was built across the river. An aqueduct so wide and big that a barge can float in it! It was necessary to cross the Oise River in order to move south, towards the Aisne.River. What a weird feeling, sailing on the "bridge" with the river below me!

Entering the tunnel.

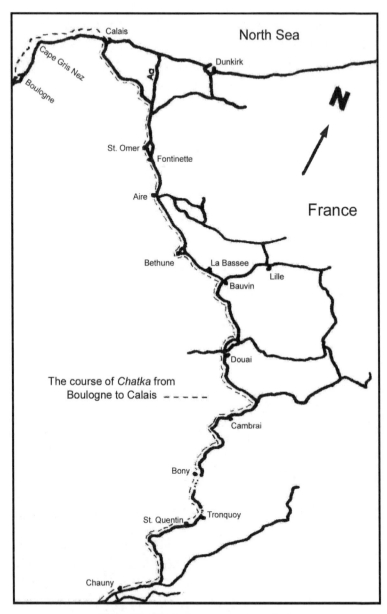

Map of the Chatka's *passage through the
maze of the northern France canals.*

I was again sailing alone during this part of the trip. Our tiny motor had a healthy appetite. Funds were disappearing fast; gasoline in France was very expensive. We decided that after Abbecourt, when the boat would be raised to the level of Canal de l'Oise a l'Aisne, Janusz would go back to Paris and try to earn some money to feed the little stinker. I did not mind this arrangement, Janusz had spent more time in Paris, and he knew people who could get him some temporary employment. The canal was relatively easy to negotiate; it was less than fifty kilometers in length and only 13 locks. I knew that the next lock, in Guny, was at a distance of eleven kilometers; *Chatka* was moored there late at night. Traffic on the canal was quite heavy, there were a number of motor-less barges that were slowly towed by locomotives moving on the rails laid on shore. With the oncoming traffic also heavy, it was sometimes necessary to wait a considerable time before it was possible to overtake a slowpoke.

Slightly more than twenty kilometers farther I was in front of another tunnel, this time medium-sized, two and a half kilometers long, more or less, where the use of an electric mule was compulsory. Nine locks more and I was at the entrance to the Canal Lateral a l'Aisne. There was some work being done on the canal, and the traffic was directed towards the Aisne River itself, partially canalized far back in time, in 1680. We were aware of it, had learned it from Peter, the skipper of *Hyperion,* but we hoped that two weeks was ample time to fix whatever had to be fixed. Hopes were for naught, I had to motor against the current for more than twenty kilometers, but as a consolation, there were no locks. It took me about ten hours to reach Berry-au-Bac, our first meeting point with Janusz that we had determined before we parted. At Barry-au-Back there is a junction point with the Canal de l'Aisne a la

Marne. A slightly different rule of orthography, but it was still a canal between the Aisne and Marne Rivers. This canal is not a busy one. Normally to enter it, it would not take any waiting. This time it was different, lots of barges were trying to exit the Aisne River, there was a tremendous traffic jam. To give you an idea how those problems were worked out: I was twenty-second in line. It took me 27 hours to finally pass the lock leading to a canal leading to Reims, where we had set up our alternative meeting point.

After finally entering the canal, the morning of November 17, the sailing was easy. It was twenty kilometers and nine locks to the inland port of Remis; I entered it the same day, in the evening. Next morning Janusz appeared. Not knowing that I had to spend such a long time in Berry-au-Bac, he rightly calculated that I should be already in Reims. Not finding me there, he walked the path next to the canal towards the Aisne River, exactly at the time when I was motoring towards Reims. It was some bad luck that we did not meet. He slept on the bench in some park and before dawn started walking back to Reims, more than a three-hour walk. At night the temperature was near freezing, and Janusz caught a cold. On top of everything he had not been able to earn much money in Paris.

Even when passing small villages during our trip through canals we were recognized as "les navigateurs solitaires," the label given us by French newspapermen, probably for a reason that we were very often compared with Alain Bombard, who was titled as the "navigateur solitaire." Of course there were two of us, therefore it was a misnomer, but somehow it stuck with us. All that work on the boat gave us a healthy appetite, which we demonstrated on many occasions when we were invited for a gala dinner, and where we were introduced as the "two solitary sailors." We coined a small private joke, calling ourselves "nawigatorzy z soliterem,"[18] which sounded vaguely similar to the French version, but had a totally different meaning.

It is quite a distance from Reims to the sea, we did not know anybody there. In a dark mood we were strolling on the quay, when somebody called us in Polish. Someone had seen me when I arrived the previous day, and there was a note about it in a local newspaper. Mr. Kolloch, the gentleman who hailed us, was an executive of the famous Heidesieck champagne house and a member of the local Yacht Club. Our very convenient mooring place was in the industrial basin on the city's northern outskirts. We remained there for a few days. Mr. Kolloch was trying to arrange some deal with an oil company to get a supply of gasoline in exchange for an advertisement, but it required such a long and complicated bureaucratic procedure that we had to give up this idea.

It really was no longer necessary. When the officials of Mr. Kolloch's Yacht Club learned of our troubles, they decided to offer us their help. On one fine, but slightly chilly morning, accompanied by Mr. Kolloch and two young French soldiers of Polish descent, we motored through the city, to the area near the Yacht Club. There was a car waiting for us, with a few jerry cans of gasoline, but also two heavy sleeping bags, some warm clothing and even some provisions! What a beautiful gesture towards fellow sailors in trouble! Our passengers disembarked, and soon *Chatka* entered the nearby lock. The following day we were in front of the next tunnel, our fourth. It was an election day and work had stopped at 3 PM. Waiting with us was a Dutch barge and our old friend, the Belgian barge *Soli Deo*. In this international company we spent a pleasant evening, enlivened by hot conversation—topic: the French

---

[18] Polish for "navigators with a tapeworm."

working habits. Everyone had complaints, bad organization, unpleasant and uncooperative officials, and an incredible amount of time spent waiting for any kind of service required from lock and bridge keepers. After dark, we took an advantage of the small size of *Chatka* and pulled our boat through a tunnel, again only about two and a half kilometers long. Because of the noise it would create we did not dare to start the motor. In the morning we passed the first of the eight locks separating us from the old (completed in 1845) Canal Lateral a la Marne. Six and a half kilometers later we were there. Then we closely followed the Marne River for almost 50 kilometers, passed the city of Chalon-sur-Marne and, after easy sailing (only eleven locks!) at the great junction of three canals in Vitry le Francois, we entered our last canal before the Saone River: Canal de la Marne a la Saone, of course.

Almost there, right? Unfortunately no. Remember there were 225 locks to pass? Our next canal was 224 kilometers in length and it has 114 locks!

When we decided to change the route of our expedition and travel through the rivers and canals of France, our consolation was the possibility of trying ourselves against Mistral, the dreaded wind blowing from the north and falling south by the valleys of Saone and Rhone. On reaching the Gulf of Lions it attains the strength of a hurricane. Farther south, it gradually weakens, and if it reaches the coast of North Africa it is almost never stronger than a breeze. It is said that it never lasts less then three days. Whenever Mistral is blowing, the temperature drops rapidly, it can bring freezing temperatures to Marseille, on the other hand the air humidity drops considerably.

On the twenty-fifth of November we had a small celebration: we passed our one hundredth lock. Even the weather cooperated, it was a fine evening, we had chosen a nice place for a cookout, only 115 locks left! But winter was coming, and we were climbing higher and higher. Again our worst enemy was the cold. Before the sleeping bag warmed up it was difficult to fall asleep, and then in the morning it was difficult to get up. At that time we would forgo nice settings on the shores and cooked inside a makeshift tent at the stern of the boat, trying to trap the meager heat of our stove. The last serving before going to sleep was a shot of cognac mixed with a glass of hot water; it warmed us somewhat and it was easier to go to sleep. I kept the stove next to my sleeping bag, and first thing after waking up I lit it and boiled some water. A shot of cognac mixed with hot water made us warm enough and the feat of exiting our sleeping bags was made bearable.

For a long time the canal was following the route of the Marne River. A few times it had crossed the river on an aqueduct. It did not matter how many times this happened, it was an unreal experience for both of us, floating above the river! We have crossed the small (about 300 meters) and comfortably wide tunnel Condes, and continued to climb until we reached the tunnel Balesmes, almost five kilometers long and very narrow, *Chatka* had less than 3 feet of space on either side. This tunnel did not have any lighting, our hurricane lamp gave better illumination than the narrow beam of a flashlight, but it was easy to be deceived by the fantastic shadows cast on the walls and the low ceiling, and the boat rubbed now and then against the wooden guards lining the sides of the tunnel. I can imagine that a barge passing through this tunnel must have rubbed those wooden guards all the time.

The traffic was minimal, on an average of two barges a day in either direction. On the other hand, in addition to the locks, there were plenty of bascules, swing and vertical lifting bridges so low that they had to be lifted, swung or raised even for our relatively small boat. Most of the lock or bridge keepers were female and, considering that we were not very pleased with the attitude of the keepers on the other canals, the ladies here surely had the upper hand in competition for nastiness. Taking into account that most of the locks and bridges were manually operated, and that we did supply the manpower to do the operation, it was an extremely rare occasion when any of those public employees rewarded us with a smile. Quite the contrary. Normally, when we docked in front of a bridge or a lock, nobody would appear, probably busy with something else. But as soon as anyone of us touched any part of the machinery, then the lady would fly out of the house, screaming something in French, something which we, gratefully, did not understand.

On one occasion Janusz started to raise the miniature bascule bridge connecting a footpath. A furious woman appeared from nowhere and started climbing it, but Janusz, positioned at the mechanism on the other bank, kept cranking the bridge open. I steered *Chatka* through the just enough opened bridge, below the screaming Frenchwoman. The whole scene was so

Chatka Puchatków *inside the canal lock.*

comical that laughter slightly impaired our movements, never-theless Janusz courteously lowered the bridge, jumped into the waiting boat, and we were again on our way.

The aged and undersized motor started to give us problems. A brass nipple at the carburetor separated, and the connecting rod had parted. Fortunately, at practically every village there was some kind of a mechanical shop, and most had welding equipment. The fees were very reasonable; it was always the price of a one liter bottle of the local wine—25 cents. On board we had a lot of tools, but those were not the tools neces-sary to service an engine. With a few wrenches we had gotten in Bethune, we had to do our best. The engine was small and of a very basic construction, and soon we knew it quite well, too well, I might add.

After the long and narrow tunnel, the canal started steeply downhill; in the seventy kilometers left to reach Saone there were 43 locks. We were already in the valley between the Alps and the Massif Central, the birthplace of the Mistral. In this area the wind did not reach its full force, but it was cold, so cold that the surface of the water started to freeze. The worst instances were in front of the locks, where the current[19] was accumulating a sizeable amount of ice. When this was hap-pening one of us had to stay in the bows and, using a heavy oar keep breaking the ice, while the other was steering the boat. When under way on the canal covered by a very thin sheet of ice, we were afraid that it could cut into the wood of

---

[19] In the canals there was practically no current, but when locks were emp-tying and filling, every time a certain amount of water was used, this water was flowing downhill. *Chatka* was filling a small part of the lock chamber, the rest was water, much more water than in the case of a barge, which was practically filling up the lock. All that water was pushing broken ice in front of our boat which at that time was descending towards Saone.

Chatka. Our fears were not confirmed; the bow wave was lifting the thin ice, breaking it and pushing it aside.

A few days later the wind changed to southerly, which brought dense fog. The air was warmer, but the boat was dripping with condensed fog and it was uncomfortable, though on the plus side the ice had disappeared. Soon after that a very cold baby Mistral was blowing again, bringing sunny and somewhat more comfortable weather. The going was tough, but we were still making progress, and on the fifth of December we were on the Saone River.

We entered the river in Heuilley just before the end of the French working day. In front of us we had a lock free passage of 27 kilometers. The weather was agreeable, the river wide and free of obstructions, the bright moon was nearby full. We decided to motor until we were close to the lock. I was scanning the river with my binoculars, Janusz was steering. After about two hours I noticed a straight, thin, dark line across the river. We could not understand what it meant, and decided to move to the right, towards the nearby shore. Unfortunately we did it too late, the current was faster than we had estimated, and the boat was thrown against the weir. That was it, that dark line. The map showed that the river was dammed, with the lock near the right shore. In reality the water level was kept up by this submerged weir. It was made of concrete and it was about a foot under the surface. The impact threw me to the bottom of the boat; fortunately neither I nor the binoculars suffered any harm. Very importantly, *Chatka* too came out without any serious damage. We carried many old tires on both sides of the boat, using them as fenders; we lowered those tires on the port side, which was against the weir, and pushed them between the boat and the concrete, but we were not able to push the boat forward, the pressure of water flowing over the weir was too great.

Obviously we had underestimated the velocity of the current. When *Chatka* was leaving the last lock, entering the river, the current was quite sluggish. Now, fighting its strength, we found that it was faster than three knots, and that was the reason why we arrived at the lock so much sooner than our estimate.

The top of the weir was flat and formed a secure path. We moved an anchor with its line as far as we could and secured the anchor against the downstream side of the weir. Using the mainsail sheet block and tackle, which gave us a fivefold advantage, we could hardly move the boat, even using all our strength. Then we rigged another block and tackle giving us a threefold advantage. Connecting the double block of that block and tackle to the hauling line of the primary rig we had a 15-fold advantage.[20] Using this contraption, one of us could move the boat without much trouble. The disadvantage was that by running the whole length of the boat with the hauling line we could move forward less than two feet. After a while, when we were closer to the shore, the current slowed considerably and the pressure of the water had lessened. It was possible to dispense with the second block and tackle and progress faster. Finally, when we reached the point where the weir was joining the wall of the lock, there was practically no current. Without any more problems but very tired, we moored *Chatka* at the entrance to the lock and turned in for whatever part of the night was left.

Next morning, when entering the lock, our motor suddenly stopped and we could not start it again. We pulled ourselves through the lock, moored downstream, and started looking for the problem. Soon we found it: the propeller shaft had parted.

---

[20] Also called luff upon luff tackle, Spanish block and tackle.

This was more serious damage than any before. Walking four kilometers to nearby Auxone we found a welding shop where the shaft was welded. After a very short time it parted again. We dropped the anchor, stepped the masts and with favorable wind sailed towards the next sizeable town, St-Jean-de-Losne. The shaft was welded again, and. this time the weld held for a longer time, but not for long time. Yet another repair, and we decided to use the motor only during maneuvers, when approaching the lock and mooring, generally speaking, we tried to use it as little as possible. The locks were spaced quite far from each other, rarely less than twenty kilometers apart. Whenever the wind was blowing from the north, we had easy sailing and it was much more pleasant (and often faster) than going under power.

There were two kinds of weather. First: the wind blowing from the north, the air cold and dry, the sky clear. Second: southerly wind, warmer, muggy, frequent rains. The southerly wind, blowing against the current was raising considerable chop, our tiny engine was often swamped; it was useful only in sheltered areas. In certain places one of the Saone shores was lined with a towing path and it was possible to pull the boat in the old, river Volga style. In the other places, when the river was shallower, we could pole *Chatka* south, against the southerly wind.

We considered that our engine was a malicious machine, it seemed that it was breaking down at the most inconvenient moments, and at the approach to Chalon-sur-Saone it outdid itself. Our friendly Dutch barge, the one which we had met for the first time while waiting to pass one of the tunnels of the Canal de l'Aisne a la Marne, was just leaving her mooring. They noticed us, slowed down and waved us to come to them and get a tow. We knew they were going to Marseille! At that very moment the propeller shaft broke again! They waited for a while, but the traffic was heavy, the current was strong, a slow "canal barge" is not a maneuverable craft, and they gave up. What a pity, in about five days we would be in Marseille.

A southerly wind kept blowing, the river was rising fast, the current was stronger and stronger. We were no longer looking for the towing path or the shallows, in order to use the method of raftsmen of yesteryear, instead, one of us was standing at the bows, the other in the stern, both with an oar mounted as a steering oar. Soon the water level was so high that the removable parts of the weirs were taken out, and the locks were closed. We were floating down the river with unaccustomed speed, at the same time, fast river barges were laboriously moving up the river, while the slow "canal barges" were waiting for a change of weather.

Taking into account all of our predicaments, it did not take us an excessively long time to pass the 251 kilometers of the Saone River, less than two weeks. The inland harbor of Lyon is situated south of the town, on the Rhone River.

The current on the Rhone was even faster than the one we had experienced on the Saone; much faster than the speed of *Chatka* under power. Very carefully, keeping close to the left shore where the harbor is located, we managed to reach the area of more slack waters and entered a well protected basin. There, to our great joy, we spotted our friends on the barge *Soli Deo*. They did not go any farther south, but immediately offered help in finding somebody who was leaving in the direction of Marseille, and who would be willing to give us a tow. Within a short time the skipper of *Soli Deo* located a fast riverboat, *Josianne;* she was leaving early the next day to Arles and her skipper agreed to tow us there. In the morning, before dawn, one of the crew came down to *Chatka* moored alongside, and demanded a ridiculous amount of money for the tow. There were rumors, that our trip was the result of

some high-stake wager. After a long discussion and consultations with the other members of the crew, they agreed to five
dollars, almost all the money we had.

River Rhone is quite dangerous, especially in the time of
flood,[21] just like it was on the eighteen of December, the time
of our departure from Lyon. *Josianne* was moving fast, but
the towline was long enough and we could steer comfortably,
nevertheless the process required a great deal of attention. The
skipper of *Josianne* for sure knew the Rhone River. From
time to time he was passing some nasty looking rocks near the
water level, over which water was gushing, by a mere few
feet. *Chatka* was passing the same rocks by the same distance.
I think that *Josianne's* skipper was playing a little game with
us. We, on the other hand, were playing it safe, one of us was
steering, the other was in the bows ready to drop the towline
in a split second.

In the end, everything went without a problem, after about
eighty kilometers the Rhone became less threatening, and sailing and steering became more relaxed. For the night we
stopped in front of the lock of Chateauneuf, a very impressive
structure. The next morning the boats were lowered 17 meters
(56 feet). Its enormous chamber easily accepted the big riverboat *Josianne* and our *Chatka,* with plenty of room to spare, a
mere twenty-four kilometers farther down the river we entered
the monster lock in Bollene. The rise and fall in this engineering marvel is 26 meters (85 feet)! Neither of those two locks
have the gates to span the total height. We entered the chamber by the gate which was extending, I estimate, about eight
feet below the water level. The gate was closed, boats were
tied to bollards receding in the walls of the chamber. Then

---

[21] Some years later more dams were built, now sailing is much easier.

whoosh, we were dropping down very fast, the water was agitated, full of eddies and small whirlpools and, very conveniently, the bollards went down with us, a very clever feature. Even the bigger lock in Bollene emptied itself in less than ten minutes. We found ourselves in the cavernous well, in front of us was a gate, it did not open all the way to the top, it had risen less then twenty feet, my estimate.

Beyond Bollene the river was broader and straighter, the current has slowed down to about four knots. Another few hours and we were in Arles. The whole trip from a little bit south of Lyon to Arles, 270 kilometers, took only about eighteen hours of actual sailing. At about eight knots it seems fast, yes, but the current was almost never slower than four knots, sometimes more, and so our average speed was only about four knots. The distance from Arles to Port-St-Luis-du-Rhone is about forty kilometers. We gave the towline in the middle of the river, and we even did not start the engine, we simply floated south with the current, and in less than five hours—still in daylight—we were at the end of our fresh water journey. It was time to start the engine and find a mooring. Neither of the tasks was easy. The left bank of the Rhone was lined with hundreds of barges moored to the shore in triple rows. The engine has started hesitantly, on one cylinder only; something new was going bad inside its guts. Somehow we managed to get inside the gap between barges, only to be thrown by the current against three bows of three barges moored alongside. It was not that bad, the current was slowed down by the other three barges moored about fifty feet up the river, and we moored securely to the shore. We walked to a nearby lock leading to the basin, already connected with the salt water of the Golfe de Fos. There, we learned that the high level of the Rhone had made it impossible to operate the lock, that all the barges were waiting for a change of weather, which was supposed to end the flood. The opinion that the water level will go down "soon" could mean that we would have to wait maybe a few days, maybe a few weeks.

The next morning we found that a few barges were moored inside a short canal, leading from Rhone to the lock, and that there was enough empty space for *Chatka*. The problem was how to bring the boat there. The current was fast and it was too risky to attempt maneuvers with an impaired engine. We would like to reconnaissance the city of Marseille but we were very leery of leaving the boat moored to the shore of the raging river. Janusz devised a method: we would wait for the night, when nobody is on the shore, move the boat to the outside barge, then he would climb on the deck with the long line (in a fact few lines joined together) and make it fast. I would tie this line to the boat, he would untie it and give me our bow line, then, slowly paying out the improvised long line, he would let the current take me in *Chatka* to the next trio of moored barges. I would then fasten our bowline, and on a given signal Janusz would go with the long line to the barge I was moored to, we repeated the whole operation until we reached entrance to the canal.

Three times the scheme was working perfectly, on the fourth, when the boat was still far from the next mooring, Janusz slipped, lost his balance and let go of the long line. I was drifting towards the shallows; not far from Port-St-Luis-du-Rhone the river is not navigable. Of course we were prepared for a possible mishap, our heavy anchor was ready, anchor line was prepared to move freely, bitter end well fastened. I dropped the anchor, its rode started to run out rapidly. Afraid that when all its length runs out, the resulting jerk could brake it, I threw myself on the line in an attempt to slow down the boat. The operation was painful, my left side was properly bruised, but it worked. The boat was securely anchored, near the canal, but more than a hundred feet from the shore. What to do next? We were too far from each other to communicate. Janusz had disappeared for a while, then I could see that he found some dilapidated little boat. The shore was littered with pieces of old lines, he collected a number of them, tied them together and fastened one end to an upstream barge. He climbed down into that little boat and let the current carry it towards *Chatka,* until nearby, using a piece of the board to steer farther from the shore he was close enough so that I could throw him a piece of line. Again *Chatka Puchatków* had a crew of two.

I hasten to explain that I know how to anchor a fast moving boat, a procedure that should be avoided whenever possible. An anchor should be lowered slowly, and when it reaches the bottom it should be dragged on the short slope, slow down the boat, then the rode should be lengthened to get the proper slope. Unfortunately I did not have the luxury of having enough time for all that.

Anyhow. We were on the boat, a southerly wind was blowing squally twenty knots, we stepped the masts and hoisted the sails. It worked, slowly, very slowly, our boat started to move up river. Janusz, in the bows, was pulling up the anchor rode. Suddenly the wind slackened and the boat was drifting, dragging the anchor that was already on a very short slope. Before Janusz could pay out enough rode to stop the boat from drifting, we were stopped by a strange contraption, a fish trap shaped like a big water mill. At that time its wheel was not in motion, it was practically covered with uprooted trees, wooden beams, planks, lines, and almost any kind of flood carried rubbish imaginable. It took us a few hours to clear out of this mess. Finally we could moor to the cleared side of the mill and we tried to pull up the anchor. It was coming up, very easily, until it was right under the bow, then it stuck. Using the block and tackle we pulled it up, inch by inch, and when it came to the surface we saw the problem: an old, rusted steel cable. By tying this cable to the boat, then lowering the anchor, it was easy to free the fluke, and letting go of the cable (with a mighty splash), we were ready to go. We hoisted the sails and watched the mooring lines. The wind freshened, the lines went slack and again, very slowly, we were moving north towards the canal. Sometimes, when the wind has slackened a little, we were moving backward, then again towards the canal entrance. Exhausted but happy, soon we were there, sheltered from the current, and we moored the boat. A nearby, at a bus stop, a conductor was fusing around. Surprised that somebody was working during the night, in France, I went up to him and innocently asked him what time it was. It was 5:30 AM; we had been working on the river for almost twelve hours.

9

Sailing to Marseille—Help of the Polish colony—Departure from Marseille—Mistral—Repairs at sea—French warship R 718—L'Adroit pursues Chatka—Algiers—French apology number 1.

---

*W*ITH *CHATKA PUCHATKÓW* securely moored near the last lock we would have to pass, after an uneasy sleep of a few hours (there was a lot of noise on the quay, buses coming and going, loud conversations) we started towards Marseille. At the beginning we walked for two hours to reach the main road Arles-Marseille, then we hitchhiked. The weather was very unpleasant, a chilly wind with intermittent rain, we were cold, soaked. Fortunately we stumbled on a Salvation Army shelter near the northern limits of the city.

It was December 23rd; there was a big Christmas dinner at the shelter. After dinner we were given a berth in the cavernous dormitory, filled with bunks, hundreds of them. Unemployed sailors accounted for a high percentage of the occupants. Around midnight a number of the officers of Salvation Army arrived to wish us "Happy Christmas," and everyone was presented with a sizeable paper bag filled with goodies: fruits, nuts, various sweets.

On the nearby bunk there was a sailor who (as I have learned later) was crewing on one of the fishing boats from Old Harbor. Exhausted, he did not even open his package, but when most of the people began to treat themselves, the noise of the torn wrappage must have given him the illusion that he was at sea. "Just like at sea, just like at sea, noise of the waves," he murmured in his sleep. Finally he woke up, found the source of the noise, sat on his bunk and started to yell, "Stop that noise, whole day I had to listen to noise of the sea, I have enough noise of the sea."

In the morning we reached the Post Office where we received a real Christmas present: letters from friends and families. The same day we met Mr. Kruk who helped us a lot; he knew of an empty flat that we could use. The flat was empty indeed, no furniture at all, that suited us very well because, after bringing the boat to Marseille, we could spread our sails and give them a real, careful overhaul.

Christmas day brought a change of weather. The southerly wind ended and the same day we arrived back in Port-St-Luis-du-Rhone. When we left this place, a mere few rainy days before, our boat resembled a wet hen, now she was perfectly dried by the blowing Mistral, blowing so strongly that our tent was torn up. Most importantly, the water level of the Rhone River was dropping fast. Next morning the lock was back in operation, barges started to leave, and soon we were docked. Remembering all those pieces of line, which Janusz had used to float a small boat to *Chatka,* we decided it would be a pity to leave them on the shore. It was easy to pick them up; they were high on dry land, where a few days ago one had to wade in cold water.

It was not necessary to go through the hassle of unstepping the masts. After checking all the rigging, which for sure could use some work, we considered it sound enough for a short sail to Port-de Bouc, on the other side of Golfe de Fos, a distance of only about seven miles. The wind was so strong (and the rigging not too sound) that we hoisted the reefed main and the mid-sized jib, and without any problems we sailed from the basin onto the open waters of the gulf. The wind had raised considerable chop and barges were sailing on a course curved to the north, seeking the protection of the shore. Not us; sailing on a close reach we were taking some spray, but believe it or not, it was a pleasure, it was a spray of salt water! After two months, *Chatka Puchatków* was again where she belonged, at sea! We were proud of ourselves, all these troubles we had, did not defeat us.

There were two ways to go. First: sail to Port-de-Bouc, then through a narrow passage to Martigues, on the Etang de Berre—a large salt water lake—then to the tunnel Rove—a huge passage under mountainous peninsula Chaine de Estaque, its southern end opening into the harbor of Marseille. The second route would be to go around Cap Couronne, and then, following the southern shores of the peninsula sail straight to the port of Marseille. We chose the first route, for a several reasons: the wind was blowing about Force 8, our rigging, as I have

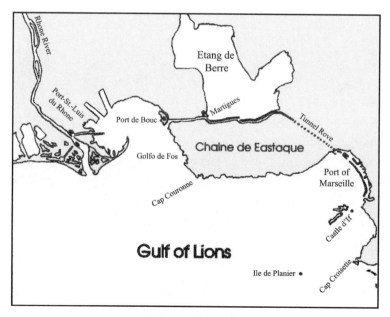

Vicinity of Marseille.

mentioned, was not in the greatest shape, and we were afraid of possible squalls next to the lee shores of Chaine de Estaque.

Then there was the second reason: we did not know Marseille, and we did not know in which part of the harbor the Yacht Club is situated. By using the tunnel Rove we would start at the northern end of the harbor and, sailing south through the whole port, we would have a good chance of spotting the Yacht Club.

After Martigues the wind started to slacken, we lost some time there, we had to wait with a few barges for the bridge to open, it was lunch brake for the bridge tender. On the lake we could see a lot of seagoing freighters, anchored and visibly not crewed, global depression of the shipping markets was visible even here.

We did not have any problems all the way up to the northern entrance of tunnel Rove.[22] Next to the southern shores of the Etang de Berre there is a passage sheltered by a series of breakwaters; it forms the last part of Canal de Marseille au Rhone. The breakwaters are not high, they are made of piled loose rocks, so we had sufficient wind for a comfortable sail. At the entrance to the tunnel we found that the towing path, a concrete shelf above water level had been destroyed by an impact of a barge and we were not allowed to pull the boat through. After unsuccessful trials to start our motor—it would sometimes start on one cylinder only—we decided to wait for a tow. It was already late and no barge has shown up until the next morning. The crew of one of the first barges that appeared, knew about us and volunteered to tow us under the peninsula.

---

[22] Tunnel Rove, more than seven kilometers (more then 23,000 feet) long, 72 feet wide and 37 feet high, it could accept large craft. Unfortunately it collapsed a few years after our passage, but as yet, nobody has blamed us.

After exiting the tunnel we sailed slowly south, but we did not notice any congregation of sailboats signaling the location of the Yacht Club. At the southern end of the commercial harbor, we reached the Old Port, supposedly founded by the Greeks from Phocaea in 599 BC. During our visit this site was not yet a primary tourist attraction, as it is today. It was a true working waterfront, a base for a multitude of small local fishing boats, and the clients of small waterfront restaurants were mostly locals. *Chatka* was moored near the entrance to this Vieux Port, in front of us was a kind of a "hole in the wall" eatery, and we decided to have something hot to eat. The menu was written in chalk on a small blackboard. We asked for the least expensive item, it was bouillabaisse. I may add that it was one of the best bouillabaisses I have ever had. The price? Less than a quarter.

The Yacht Club was farther south, slightly more than three miles. We arrived there under sails, docked at an empty space.

Under tow.

It is a normal courtesy that the skipper of an arriving boat announces the arrival and asks if the boat can remain in her present location. When the club's harbormaster saw our boat, he decided that her appearance was not good enough to be moored in his prestigious club. I can hardly blame him for this opinion; it required a good imagination to recognize that the sides of *Chatka* were at one time painted white. A lifeboat, by her nature, does not have elegant lines, but after 225 locks, six tunnels, adventures on the rivers Saone and Rhone, she did not present herself too properly. Fortunately the Vice-Commodore of the club was present. He was well informed about our expedition, calmed the harbormaster, and ordered him to let us use any facilities we may require.

From day one we were under the kind care of the local Polish colony, especially Mr. Kruk. We received some supplies, and painting the *Chatka* was the first task completed. Soon she was in her new white coat. Whenever the weather was dry, we were working on the boat, checking and repairing the rigging. During rainy days we were in the empty flat repairing the sails. New Years eve was lonely but we did not complain, that evening the last stitches were applied to the last patches. Soon we were ready, as much as our scant resources allowed; for example, we could not replace the running rigging, some lines and halyards were well used. We were waiting for a Mistral, the wait was not too long; soon the French forecasters announced that a strong Mistral is approaching. On the last evening before leaving, when we were making final checks of the boat moored in the Yacht Club, Madame Tarasiewicz[23] visited us, asked me to consider her an aunt and wished us a good trip.

---

[23] Tarasiewicz is not a common name, even in Poland. To find Tarasiewicz in Marseille was a great surprise.

On the fourth of January, just before nine in the morning, some of our newly found Polish friends wished us a good trip and, under oars—it was almost dead calm—we moved the boat to the "official" spot where our seamen's books were stamped by an immigration clerk. Among people seeing us off was a photographer from the local newspaper. I think that he was the source of our future troubles.

The little rocky isle crowned by castle d'If, of Dumas' Count of Monte Christo fame, was already north of us, we had to pass some other islands west and south off Cap Croissete. It took us a considerable amount of time to pass those nearest Marseille, then the wind became stronger, we lowered the mizzen, and when the last island was abeam we had to change the standard main for a storm sail.

Maybe it was this press photographer who was making pictures of our departure, maybe it was someone else who had seen *Chatka* sinking, soon after leaving Marseille. If we shall give that someone the benefit of a doubt, maybe he saw us disappearing behind one of the islands. Maybe when we lowered the mainsail, he thought that the sail had disappeared, because the boat foundered, but my strong suspicion is that he wanted to sell his pictures at a good price. One way or another, news about our demise was published the same day in the Marseille's evening paper, *La Provancal*. Many French newspapers, including those in Paris reprinted this dramatic news. *PAP*[24] wired it to Poland, and the crazy rumor here had become big news there, in Poland.

Staszek Mioduszewski, himself once working as a sailor was concerned and telephoned Inscription Maritime in Mar-

---

[24] Polska Agencja Prasowa (Polish Press Agency).

Leaving Marseille.

seille. When asked about *Chatka Puchatków* and her crew, Monsieur Inspecteur became very excited:

"Ils son fous!"[25] He was shouting into the telephone.

When asked how strong was the storm, about the wind direction:

"It was very bad weather, it was very bad weather." The Inspector was repeating over and over.

"Did any of your ships sink during this storm?"

"Our ships never sink, because our ships never leave the harbor during a storm."

Staszek, himself the sailor, did not conduct any further inquiry.

Earlier I had given a brief description of the Mistral, it was correct, but it should be added, that when proper atmospheric conditions are present it blows not only down the Rhone Valley (between Massif Central and Alps), but also down the Garone Valley (between Massif Central and Pyrenees). In that case the behavior of the storm can be described as a "fight" between two winds: one almost exactly northern, blowing from the Rhone Valley and another, northwesterly, from the Garone Valley. The interaction of these two winds creates a storm of very strong winds with variable directions from north to almost directly west.

This kind of storm creates very confused seas, for which the Gulf of Lions is famous. Those seas can be dangerous even for big ships, and especially for big ships, when the crew may have difficulty keeping a safe course, and the hull can be damaged.

"Our" Mistral was just of this kind. I cannot describe the next few days as particularly enjoyable, but compared to our experiences in the English Channel it was much less danger-

---

[25] "They are madmen."

ous. The sea was very deep, and therefore the waves were not as steep as the ones we encountered in the north. Also, the changing direction of the stormy wind did not allow the creation of big trains of high seas which could produce a rogue wave. The only disadvantage was that the use of a sea-anchor (if it were necessary) was not a practical alternative.

The wind forecast was Force 11, the same strength we experienced in the English Channel. In reality it was stronger, I have experienced a few storms of Force 12, and this was stronger. Not all the time, of course, but we have had a "prolonged squall" lasting a few hours when we could not carry a stitch of sail and under bare poles *Chatka* was doing about five knots.

There were problems. First to go was the halyard of the mainsail, the one we were worrying about. Initially it did not create much of a problem. I tied a block to the mast, as high as I could reach (I was taller), it was high enough for the double-reefed storm main. The second was a block of a running back stay: it disintegrated, but that was easy to fix, there were spare blocks on the boat. Then the yard of the storm mainsail had broken, again it was not much of a problem. Soon we were only under "red" storm jib. We could not carry it for long, because it developed violent Carnot[26] eddies. We were afraid for our mast and therefore changed it for a "pink jib," our smallest, an area of less than five square feet.

Night had come, it was Janusz's turn to keep watch, and I went to sleep. About two hours later I was awakened by

---

[26] When wind is blowing close to perpendicular to the sail (boat runs with the wind) the air flow on the lee side of the sail is not laminar but perturbed. When the wind is strong enough an eddy can form, and distort the sail, creating the conditions to start an eddy in another part of the sail. The stronger the wind, the faster changes will occur, and lead to violent vibrations.

the noise of a nearby engine and Janusz's loud shouts. That was a close call. A sizeable freighter has passed nearby, behind our stern.

Frequent changes of wind direction were beneficial in terms of keeping the height of the seas lower, on the other hand it made the job of the helmsman difficult and tiring. The standard four-hour watches were too long, so we started changing every two hours. The boat was taking almost no water, but with the wind of this strength, the air was full of salty spray and our old, battered oilskins were offering a scant protection. We had a Russian military type square piece of rubberized canvas that could be used as a poncho, and that was assigned to the helmsman. Sleeping was done in a sitting position, on the floorboards under the cover of a sail. It was cold; cold was our enemy number one when we were sailing up north, and now in the cold Mistral.

Next day, January the fifth, the wind was strongest, that was a day when we were sailing a few hours under bare poles, and the rest of the day under the "pink" jib. Not much can be said about a day like that, we had to concentrate on two important tasks at hand: to be very alert and sail the boat as well as we could, and secondly, to preserve our strength because Mistral could blow for another few days more.

Time was on our side, the farther south we were, the less violent the wind would be. Anyhow the wind was from the proper direction, and every hour that passed we were closer to the African shores and warmer weather. On the sixth of January it was possible to change the jib for our standard "red" storm jib and the reefed storm mainsail (we replaced the broken yard with an oar). The seas calmed considerably and I was contemplating climbing the mainmast and replacing the halyard. Breaking the rule (I was disturbing his rest, it was not an emergency) I called Janusz to steer the boat for a while, but having taken advantage of milder weather he was asleep so heavily that he did not answer my calls. It was not like Janusz and it made me a little worried. Unfortunately the seas soon increased and the opportunity was lost. It was a pity, if it would be possible to hoist the yard higher, for sure we could have shaken out the reefs and increased *Chatka's* speed.

On the fourth day after leaving Marseille the sun was shining, and when the boat was on top of a wave the horizon was visible, and we could shoot the sun during its culmination. Our latitude was close to 40 degrees north, the Balearic Islands were abeam. The seas were confused, the wind not strong enough for the sails we could hoist (jib, reefed main, mizzen), but we could sail south-southwest comfortably. Despite wild rocking I have managed to climb the mainmast and thread the piece of thin steel cable through the halyard block. It was a very demanding job and in a short time every one of my muscles was aching, I had to give up and leave the free piece of cable dangling a few feet from the topmast. Next day the storm returned, it was blowing about Force 8, the horizon disappeared, we could not check our latitude, and again we could not replace the halyard. A small octopus launched itself from a steep wave, it was probably escaping from something, and it ended up in the reefed mainsail. It was so small, not enough for even a meager meal, so I threw it back into the sea.

Finally! Finally, on the ninth of January we managed to replace the halyard. The seas were calm enough that we were able to unstepp the mast. For this operation we wanted to steer exactly with the waves. Only the mizzen was available, and holding that course would mean possible jibing. To get around this problem we jury-rigged the square sail, hoisted on the mizzenmast. While I was steering, Janusz unstepped the mainmast, checked all the rigging, stepped the mast back, and hoisted the standard mainsail,[27] the standard jib, and the mizzenmast got its standard sail. We were very soon rewarded, at about 8 PM Janusz spotted the glare of a lighthouse on the African coast.

When we were planning our trip, we did not take into account the possibility of sailing the Mediterranean. We therefore did not have any charts of that region. Over the years I had collected thousands of nautical charts of practically the whole world; they were catalogued and stored in my parents' house. When we decided to change the route, I asked my stepfather, also a sailor, to send part of the Western Mediterranean folio to Marseille. Those charts were outdated, so we bought a current French general chart of this area. It gave us the up-to-date location and characteristics of the main lighthouses. That was a very good move, because after five days of a heavy storm we were not in the possession of anything what could be described as an "accurate position."

During the night, we were closing on the shore, and I was sure that the lighthouse was Gp. Fl. (2) ev. 10 sec. There were a few possibilities: lighthouses on the African shore were positioned in a repetitive series: (counting from east) Fl. ev. 5 sec. Gp. Fl. (2) ev. 10 sec. Gp. Fl. (3) ev. 15 sec. then the same again, starting with Fl. ev. 5 sec. The distances between lighthouses varied and if we could see another light our position would be well established. The wind was light and variable. During my night watch it veered, in less than one hour, more than 300 degrees! It was difficult to keep exact dead reckoning, but we had to do it in order to identify the next light. Finally there it was! Consternation—the characteristic Gp. Fl. (3) ev. 20 sec. should not have been here! The new French

---

[27] Our mainsails, standard and storm, were attached to their own yards.

map gave us the answer—it was a new lighthouse. The first light we saw was Cap Bougaroun, we were much farther east than we had thought.

Close to midnight, January eleventh to twelfth, we were approached by an unknown vessel. She trained on us a very bright searchlight, which was completely blinding us, and she was keeping near our stern. Janusz decided to illuminate the whole scene with one of our flares, but those we kept handy were swollen by a few days of air saturated with spray, and could not fit into the gun. Of course we should have checked them, but being preoccupied with repairs, and with previously our not well known position, finally glad to get a good rest, we did not. I was still in my sleeping bag, swearing at the interruption of my sleep. *Chatka* was not far from the shore, and I suspected that it was a customs patrol boat. Before Janusz could get dry flares, a very loud voice, obviously through a megaphone, had asked in perfect Polish:

"Co to za jednostka?"[28]

In a second I was out of my sleeping bag.

"Hurrah! It is the lifeboat *Chatka Puchatków*." At the same time I was hoisting our flag.

"Do you need help?"

"Thank you, no."

"Where are you heading?"

"To Oran."

"Do you know your position?"

"Naturally, approximate. May I ask what ship is it?"

A voice had answered, but neither of us could understand, not even after a repetition.

"Do you need anything?"

---

[28] What ship?

Since we were sure that we were speaking with a Polish merchant ship, I answered:

"If you have too much grub, you can give us some."

The ship came closer, too close in fact, her bow broke the starboard rear shroud of the mainmast and opened the hook of the front starboard shroud turnbuckle.

It was not a Polish ship, it was a French man-of-war with the hull number R 718. At night we took her for a destroyer, but it was possible that she was something smaller, in the darkness we could easily misjudge her size. They lowered some sea biscuits and some canned food, and disappeared into the dark. Using the surviving shroud as a starboard rear and exchanging turnbuckle we steadied the mainmast, hoisted the sails, and we too were on our way.

As I had mentioned, during the first days of sailing near the African coast the weather was very unsettled. We soon observed the pattern—not long after sunset, every night we were drenched by short-lived, heavy rains, frequently accompanied by strong, squally wind. The next night after our encounter with R 718, the squall was so strong that as a precaution we lowered the main. Raindrops were so large that their splashes into the sea were producing small rings of fluorescence. The wind raised tiny, breaking wavelets, their tiny combs were also fluorescing, as a result the whole sea around us was white, even our boat was somewhat illuminated.

The next day a regular pattern of land and sea breezes developed, at sunrise the wind was blowing from the land (land breeze), it was becoming lighter and lighter, at about ten in the morning it was replaced by a dead calm. Two hours later, around noontime, the sea breeze (wind from the sea towards shore) was starting to blow, its strength increasing all the time until about three in afternoon. It was holding steady for about two hours, then it was diminishing and about ten at night it was calm again for about two hours. Around midnight the land breeze was starting, and lasted until midmorning.

This kind of sailing, not very fast but it was most enjoyable. First of all, it was warm, maybe even too warm, but we did not mind it because for once we did not suffer in the cold weather. The slow current was against us, but even this did not spoil our good humor, it was like pleasure sailing. The good times lasted until we were west of Algiers, then two, three more days and we should be in Oran, our next destination, and the next package of mail. But then the weather changed, we got westerly wind Force 6, maybe slightly more. Thanks to the contrary current, we could hardly hold our longitude. There was no any reason to beat to the west, we could get shelter and wait out the westerly wind behind Cap de la Pointe Pescade, in a wide bight where port of Algiers is located. When we were close to the shore, about seven miles, the wind slackened to about Force 5, but the seas were still steep and bothersome.

While sailing towards the Cap de la Pointe Pescade we noticed a French man-of-war, something like a frigate, moving fast in our direction. After a short time she arrived, kept to our lee, lowered the rope ladder, and using a megaphone ordered us to come alongside. To anyone with any knowledge of the sea, it would be obvious that docking in such conditions, on the windward side of a large (comparing to *Chatka Puchatków*) vessel, would end in disaster. At that time in Algeria, a war was simmering, we figured that the Frenchman wanted to inspect our boat.

I yelled to them that let's move behind the cape, where the waters are calmer. They did not pay any attention to our suggestion, and they attempted to dock with *Chatka* with their windward side. When the frigate's bow was just a few yards from us, we jibed and sailed in the other direction. Passing near our pursuer again I tried to convey to them both in English and my poor French, our concerns about the danger of the docking.

The short and beamy *Chatka* made a 180-degree change of course in a few seconds, but it took the long man-of-war a much longer time. Once on the new course, they were next to us in practically no time, the whole maneuver lasted about fifteen minutes. When they were close to us again, we jibed again, and again, and again. But for the danger to the boat, we surely could have enjoyed that play. The Frenchman's first approach was about two hours before sunset, it was getting dark, and we were still in the game, still trying to convince him to move toward the shore. In reality we were trying to move toward the cape but the wind was increasing, it was already blowing Force 6, and we were still under full sail.

After our encounter with the R 718 we had repaired our mainmast shrouds as well as we could, but probably not well enough for this wild ride in the increasing wind. During one of the jibes we lost the mainmast. It took very little time to pull the whole mess into the boat, unstepp the mizzenmast, and stepp it in the place of main. We were ready to hoist the reefed mainsail when a loud crack announced the arrival of the Frenchman. Once more we were presented with a rope ladder and a beaming officer invited us to climb aboard. When we categorically refused, the officer and the group of sailors accompanying him were visibly surprised. We already knew man-of-war's name, we saw it on a small plaque on the side of a superstructure, it was *L'Adroit*[29] (hull number 644).

We were trying to save our boat. *Chatka* was being thrown against the steel hull, a strong wind was pushing us against it, and we were breaking one by one all pieces of wood we had

---

[29] "Skillful," quite a misnomer.

on board, trying to keep the vessels apart. Lying parallel to the waves, narrow hull of the man-of-war was rocking violently, her rubrail, a wooden beam 10 x 20 inches, was pushing again and again *Chatka's* side underwater. Soon our boat was full of water, her port side was in a horrible state.

We were trying to communicate in English, but there was nobody on board of *L'Adroit* who could speak any English. They also did not understand much of my French, no surprise here. In desperation I shouted:

"Est quelqu'un qui parle Polonais?"[30]

Consultations on board *L'Adroit*. It appears that yes, some cadet named Kowalski. In a few minutes he is at the side. His Polish is not fantastic, but we do not have any problem communicating. He does not understand what the whole fuss is about. We are being rescued by the brave French sailors, why we do not want to come onboard, to the comfort of *L'Adroit?*

Our boat was in the process of being destroyed, we did not want any discussion, just a short explanation of what our thoughts were about the "rescue operation." The cadet Kowalski had left to convey the news to the skipper. Soon he was back with the skipper's question:

"What should I do now?"

"Tow us to Algiers."

"To Algiers? Why to Algiers?"

"Because it is nearest."

After a few more minutes, which for us was the equivalent of an eternity, the French lowered two sailors with a portable two way radio, and started to tow us towards the lights of the nearby Algiers. Luckily, the skipper, probably himself slightly scared by the destruction caused by the "rescue," heeded my

---

[30] "Does anybody speak Polish?"

request to keep the towing speed below three knots, other-wise the damaged *Chatka* would turn into an impersonation of a submarine. We did not have to bail out the boat, the water level was well below the benches. The port side was so dam-aged that thanks to the flotation tanks the excess water had flown outside.

We were flabbergasted by the "seamanship" of the French. Or maybe it was a case of simple stupidity. During the two hours we were trying to avoid the boarding, we were in obvi-ous control of the boat, so how was it possible to think that we were in need of help? Even if they did not understand English or our French, our gestures and actions should have been quite unmistakable.

While under tow for almost three hours, the French Navy headquarters in Algiers were informed how the "rescue mis-sion" was conducted. Outside the breakwater, a towline was passed to a small tugboat, two torpedo boats positioned them-selves on both sides of *Chatka Puchatków,* and in such a decorous way we entered the French naval base in Algiers. On the quay the skipper of *L'Adroit,* a French lieutenant com-mander, was waiting to tell me that he was sorry. I am glad that his English was negligible, because I was trying to con-vince him, that maybe he would make a good priest, but surely sailoring was not his calling. Taking into account the events of that day, I think that I should be excused.

10

*French apology number 2—False alarm—
m/s Piłsudski—Rescue operations—French repair
the damage—Cherchell—Repairs and cures in
Cherchel—Shopping trip to Algiers—s/s Wisła—
Levanter—Riding the waves.*

OUR CEREMONIAL ENTRANCE to the port of Algiers was taking place well after ten in the evening. Then there was a big dinner in the Navy headquarters. There were no less than twenty naval officers and plenty of newspapermen. For the first time we had the opportunity of trying the excellent Algerian rose, a wine that has rightly deserved its great fame.

During the dinner, an officer, an adjutant to the commander of the base, made a formal speech. He "expressed regret" about the "unfortunate occurrence" and assured us that the naval shipyard will make all necessary repairs to alleviate all the damage done by the action of *L'Adroit*.

We learned about the "rescue action" by the French authorities. Because of a false alarm made in Marseille, they were looking for wreckage of the *Chatka Puchatków* in the wrong place. After the accidental "discovery" by R 718, they assumed that we must be short of food. When *L'Adroit* spotted us again, she was ordered to "rescue" us. For some reason our meeting with R 718 was not reported in the press. Big headlines "DISCOVERED!" had appeared only after the encounter with *L'Adroit*.

We had received telephone calls from Poland, suddenly there was no problem with money, we were promised that 250 dollars would be immediately wired to Algeria.

I have to admit that the shipwrights in the naval shipyard were excellent. In the morning our boat was out of the water, and under our supervision all the equipment, sails, two months' supply of canned food was removed and stored safely. Two groups of carpenters were assigned to the boat, one to make a new mainmast, another to repair the badly damaged port side. To facilitate the work the flotation tanks were removed. To our dismay, even they did not escape damage, two of them were holed.

Obviously the French Navy knew about (and employed) spin doctors. After a few days we received a transcript of the commentary of Radio Paris. It was published in Polish newspapers:

"The situation became almost tragic. Luckily for the sailors, the French authorities once having found Chatka Puchatków, *kept her under constant observation. Surveillance aircraft and patrol ships were following every movement of the minute boat. Having discovered that* Chatka Puchatków, *because of her broken mast, was at the mercy of the waves and winds, the French Admiralty sent a patrol boat, which reached the sailors. This time the help was not refused. The thrown towline was caught, and* Chatka Puchatków *was towed to the port of Algiers. The Polish sailors will be there not less than three days. That time is necessary not only for completing the repairs of the lifeboat, but also for the completely exhausted Poles to be back in a good form."*

It is understood, that the function of the Navy is not to save lives, quite the contrary I may add, nevertheless some seamanship training would not hurt. I had read an account of an attempted retrieval of oceanographic scientific gear intention-

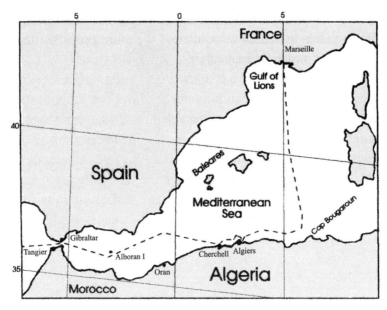

The course of Chatka *from Marseille to the Atlantic Ocean.*

ally dropped by a helicopter close to a light aircraft carrier.[31] The first motor whaleboat launched was smashed against the side of the carrier. A second boat ended up hanging vertically on her bow fall, spilling her crew into the water. A third boat managed to rescue the crew of the second boat, but her falls became so tangled that she could not be hoisted and was warped into a side loading port. The gear was not recovered.

Practice makes perfect. The Coast Guard undertakes spectacular rescue operations almost every day, very often in the most difficult of conditions. I know about another Rescue of the crew that abandoned the torpedoed and sinking Polish

---

[31] William G. Van Dorn, *Oceanography and Seamanship,* Dodd, Mead & Co. 1974.

ocean liner *m/s Piłsudski*. My stepfather, first radio officer Maksymilian Strzeliński, was there; I therefore know the story quite well from an eyewitness.[32]

During November of 1939, in Newcastle, *m/s Piłsudski* was converted into a troop carrier and on November 25 left the harbor for her destination to Australia, at that time she was manned by only a skeleton crew. Her course was near the English coast, on waters that were declared safe of the enemy; she was proceeding without an escort, and was supposed to meet her Navy guardian farther south. An enterprising skipper of a German U-Boat positioned his submarine near the shore, not far from Framborough Head. His two torpedoes hit *Piłsudski* shortly before dawn on the first night of her voyage when she was near Hull. The sea conditions were rough, but all necessary lifeboats were launched successfully. It appeared that all personnel were in the boats, only the captain and the first officer who had lowered the last lifeboat, were still on deck.

The first officer descended to the waiting lifeboat, while the captain had decided to have another look and has found two young mess boys who were in their bunks close to the point of impact of one of the torpedoes. They had both lost consciousness and came to when the cold water reached them. They managed to find their way in the darkness and heard the captain's calls who found yet another crew member, a cook, and they were all preparing to launch a raft.

It was a bad time for the British Navy. On September 17th, the fleet carrier *HMS Courageous* was sunk in the Irish Sea.

---

[32] I knew another survivor of that tragedy. My professor of astronavigation in the Marine Academy was Cpt. Karol Borchardt, in November 1939 serving as first officer on *m/s Piłsudski*. About thirty years later he wrote the best-seller *I mean, the Captain* (*Znaczy Kapitan* in Polish) dedicated to the memory of Captain Stankiewicz, commandant of *Piłsudski* during her last voyage.

On October 14, a German U-Boat managed to penetrate the Naval Base in Scapa Flow and torpedoed the battleship *Royal Oak*. She sunk with the loss of 833 people. Rumors were rampant. If the battleship, designed to take heavy punishment sunk in 3 minutes[33] what about the merchant vessel? As I had mentioned, *Piłsudski* was torpedoed not long before sunrise, when, with the exception of the watch on the bridge and the mechanics on duty in the machine room, everyone was asleep. With those 3 minutes in mind, people rushed from their cabins, in various different states of undress, and, what was more important without shoes. The passages were littered with broken glass, and most of the people running towards lifeboats injured their feet. Another problem was that in the hurried atmosphere the census was not taken, or rather could not be taken.

Piłsudski was listing heavily to the port and the captain, afraid that the ship could capsize at any minute, decided to launch the raft. The mess boys were terrorized with fear and refused to jump into the sea. The captain then jumped first, as an encouragement, the boys followed him soon after, only the cook could not muster enough courage to jump. Finally, in the darkness, they thought that they saw him jumping, but they could not see him in the water. Anyway, soon the waves took the unwieldy raft farther away, separating them from the ship. It was a cold late November night in the North Sea. All three were on top of the raft, out of water, but the wind was cold and they were thoroughly wet.

Soon the British destroyer was on the scene, people on the raft were rescued first, then survivors in the lifeboats. No boat was overcrowded, one had only one passenger: the cook. He had simply hidden himself in the lifeboat that was ready to be

---

[33] Actually she sank in 13 minutes.

launched, but because everybody was already accommodated, she was left on her rosters. *Piłsudski* did not turn turtle, quite the contrary. Before sinking she settled on the even keel, and when the water came high enough so that the lifeboat with the cook inside could float, she gently floated away.

Here accounts start to differ. According to some, the only casualty was the captain who was rescued alive, but later died of the combination of exposure and heart failure. According to others the fourth mechanic fell overboard from a lifeboat when he lost his balance while removing glass from his foot and he could not be found; if that version can be believed, he probably injured himself during the fall.

The crew of a British destroyer performed brilliantly. Everyone was taken from the water, despite the rough weather there were no serious injuries during the rescue operation.

Taking into account that *m/s Piłsudski* was a sister ship of *m/s Batory,* built in the same Italian shipyard, launched about only half a year later, it is very probable that the lifeboats on both liners were of the same construction. If you will remember, *Chatka Puchatków* was an old lifeboat taken from *Batory.*[34] Incredible as it sounds, but it seems that my stepfather was in an almost identical lifeboat, as I was years later, sailing the same North Sea.

We had a busy time in Algiers. Besides spending a lot of time in the naval shipyard, we were entertained by the members of the Algerian Yacht Club who were showing us beautiful Algiers;[35] a mixture of European and an Arabic city. Wide avenues of the "lower city" bordering the spacious port, small

---

[34] Replaced by an ugly plastic tub, requiring much less work to keep her seaworthy.

[35] This was true during our visit. I have read opinions of more recent visitors: the city is dirty and neglected. Entering the Casbah is a suicidal act.

exotic streets of the old Casbah situated on the hills of "upper city." Lots of marine history; it got its prominence when the pirate Barbarossa made his base in Algiers; it became the Barbary pirates' lair for the next three centuries until the United States navy captain Stephen Decatur, in 1815, forced free passage for American vessels. Not long after that, the pirate fleet was totally destroyed by the Anglo-Dutch force. It was a base for the Free French during the Second World War.

In the evenings there were splendid dinners at the French Naval Headquarters, where we had to tell about our adventures over and over again. We were in practically constant communication with Poland, the promised 250 dollars were continuously "on the way," but still did not reach Algiers. On the 19th of January we noticed a strange goings-on at the base; people at the shipyard started to hurry up, we did not even have a chance to check the boat thoroughly, when all our supplies were brought from the warehouse. Our boat was launched, and we were trying to stow everything in the order that we were used to, because it is most unnerving to have to search the boat for misplaced items. We took a break for lunch, during which the French officer paid us a visit and announced (I quote literally):

"Your boat is repaired. You must this evening go from Algiers. It is order of Commandant."

We never learned the reason for this change of atmosphere. Maybe something was about to happen on the base, some movement of men-of-war, whatever. One way or another, two hours later the same small tugboat that had towed us into the harbor, pulled us out of the harbor. This was not very convenient for us, because we had still not received "our" money and we wanted to buy some supplies before leaving. But we had already felt the might of the French Navy, and for sure we did not have much to say.

Not long after we were on our own, a pleasant breeze became near gale, the new mast started to vibrate in an unsettling way, and we had to change the mainsail and jib for storm sails. The wind was blowing from the shore, the seas were minimal and we had a nice speed. Before midnight we were well beyond Cap de la Pointe Pescade with its Fl. ev. 5 sec. lighthouse, the wind moderated, and we could again return to our standard suit of sails. Previously, we were sailing on the port tack, the seas were small and our port side above water line was always above the water level. When the wind calmed and the waves increased, we noticed that *Chatka* started taking water. It was not easy to determine the source of the leak; finally it was obvious that the port side of the lifeboat was water- tight only below the water line. The leak was considerable; one bucket every three minutes; it would be very difficult to make the repairs at sea. To work from the outside (always the preferred approach) one would have to hang overboard; to do it from inside, the flotation tanks would have to be removed. At that time we were about 10 miles from Cherchell, an ancient port about 40 miles west of Algiers. That was a bad day onboard *Chatka:* on top of the unpleasant discovery of a not very wholesome repair—probably because authorities were rushing the carpenters—we had lost a hat, a can opener, and a chart. Those were the first and only items we lost overboard during the whole trip. Then the final and worst happening: Janusz's feet became very swollen and painful. This affliction had already been troubling him from time to time for a while. First, it was during the Mistral, when he was unexplainably hesitant to help me with the mast, then again he was complaining during the last two days in Algiers, but at those times the discomfort was minor. Near Cherchell the situation turned bad, he suffered terribly. Obviously having his feet in the water (when bailing out the boat) had triggered this attack.

Chatka Puchatków *arrives in Cherchell.*

It is difficult to imagine, but it took us three and a half days to sail those 10 miles that separated us from Cherchell. During those days we were plagued by calms and very light and variable winds. It was impossible to continuously bail the boat. Janusz could not do it, and from time to time I also needed a rest. He was steering most of the time while I did all the other chores. As a result, most of the time we had some water in the boat, she was sluggish, and the light airs we experienced hardly moved her. During the night a strong current pushed us almost fifteen miles back towards Algiers. After that we were hugging the shore, trying to hold onto any hard-won mile. Unknown to us we were near an area of heavy fighting. Practically all the time we could hear the sound of gunfire in the nearby mountains. At one point when we were near some headland, somebody sent a burst of machine fire in our direction, the bullets were singing quite close. Most probably it was a warning not to come nearer, but we did not wait for an explanation. With the light offshore breeze we mowed towards open water as fast as we could, but for sure we would have liked to move much faster.

In the last day, before reaching Cherchell, when I had already figured out the vagaries of local weather and local currents and we were close to the harbor, we were approached during the afternoon calm by a few natives in a small motorboat who offered to tow us to Cherchell. When we explained that we did not have any money to pay for their services, they made sure that the boat was Polish, and in a very friendly manner they assured us that they did not expect any payment and insisted on giving us a tow. Finally we decided to accept their offer and started to prepare the boat for a tow. At that moment, from behind a mountain appeared a French attack plane, flying very low, it was above us in the matter of seconds. The crew of the small motorboat was more alert than we were—when we looked in their direction they were a few hundred feet from us, moving away at full speed.

Before sunset at about 6 PM, we were safely moored at the quay in Cherchell. We were informed that at 8 PM the whole town, harbor including, was under curfew. We did not have anything to do, in the dark it was impossible to start repairing the leak, we had to wait until the next day. One thing was comforting, no more bailing. The surface in the quiet harbor was totally smooth, and *Chatka* was not taking any water. We were slightly annoyed by our slow progress. We declared that our next port of call would be Oran, but having had enough of the French bureaucrats, we made the decision to sail directly to Tangier, outside of the French jurisdiction. We should have been approaching Tangier right now. Instead we were docked in Cherchell, again in a French-controlled territory.

At that time there was a strong garrison of the French Foreign Legion there. In the morning we were greeted by a Polish legionnaire. He was attached to the French Officers Academy located in Cherchell. After being informed of Janusz's health problem, he arranged a visit to the Academy physician. He was a young man; before he was drafted he worked as a physician on Jacques Costeau's ship *Calypso*. Small world!

Monsieur Maire[36] of Cherchell declared us the guests of the city and insisted that a physician of the city hospital be involved in the Janusz's cure. The duo was working very well, soon the swelling and pain were gone, but according to their professional opinion Janusz should rest for at least

---

[36] Mr. Mayor.

a week. All that time he was housed in the sick bay of the Officers Academy. I was kept busy repairing the boat. First I removed flotation tanks on the port side. Using the block and tackle I gave the boat a list to the port. From inside it was easy to see the sources of the leaks; there were six of them! Then I moved the boat in such a way that she was moored to the quay on her starboard. From the locals I borrowed a small wooden dinghy and, working from the outside, I was able to easily fix all the leaks.

Cherchell would be a nice small town if not for the overwhelming presence of the military. They were everywhere, I was trying to take excursions outside the city walls (yes the city was walled, the gates were closed at the onset of the curfew), the roads were heavily patrolled. Another eyesore were the literally thousands of broken ancient columns, cornices, other architectural fragments difficult to identify, stacked at every public square, actually at every empty place. The sources of all that precious junk were archeological digs conducted all around the area, and findings were abundant. Cherchell is an old city, founded in the fourth century BC by the Phoenicians. For a long time it was the capital of Mauretania, then came the Roman Period, then it was a part of the Byzantine Empire. According to the local lore there is a big part of an ancient city, together with its harbor, sunk in the sea, when an earthquake caused the shore to submerge more than a hundred feet. If one goes in the boat just outside the present day port, they say, that on a quiet day one can see immense white buildings under the water (we did not see any).

It was very difficult to get a telephone connection with Poland; on the other hand it was very easy to call Paris. I made arrangements to call collect the Polish Press Agency in Paris, and they would then relate the message to Poland. As usual, our main concern was money. Soon I learned that money had not yet been sent to a bank in Algiers and I asked that they would redirect the money to a bank in Cherchell.

After the boat was fixed, tanks put in place, all the small repairs done; I had plenty of time to explore the city. Everywhere I was warmly welcomed by the locals, whenever somebody was cooking (and a lot of cooking was done in the open) I was invited to participate. Some dishes were better than others, but all were exotic. Heavily spiced, they mainly consisted of lamb and some grain; desserts were incredibly sweet but with a pleasant flavor. Invariably, we had dinners with the Legionnaires in the Officers' Academy. There was only one Pole, but quite a few Czecks, Slovaks, and British.

We received that famous 250 dollars on the eighth day of our stay in Cherchell. Next day we took the bus to Algiers to buy some supplies, not available locally. It was only a 40-mile ride; and it took a little over an hour. We bought some lines, new oilskins, a new lantern, some odds and ends. It was amazing how the prolonged war had affected the countryside. Young amputees were seen everywhere, fields left unattended, fashionable seaside houses boarded up. It was easy to see that not much love was lost between the French and the Arabs. One example: the bus stopped to pick up a fat, sweaty Frenchwoman, the bus was full, we were standing. In the front row an Arab teenager was sitting; he had a pair of crutches, one leg was gone. The French matron said something to him in Arabic, and without a word, the boy get up and gave up his seat.

During most of the whole time we spent in Cherchell the weather was beautiful and sunny, the temperature agreeable and a nice fresh wind from the east. We returned from Algiers and the same day left the harbor, escorted by a boat with the newsreel crew and our Polish friend from the Officers' Academy. With a westerly wind we were steering due north, in order to gain some sea room, then the wind changed to a pleasant eastern and we were making good progress. Not for long, unfortunately, the next day brought variable winds and frequent rainy squalls. We almost enjoyed this weather. Donning our new oilskins, we could keep ourselves dry and comfortable. In the afternoon, the wind stabilized on a westerly direction and was gaining strength. There was no reason to work hard and to try to beat against the rising storm. We had dropped the sea anchor, but it did not work well; only after we hoisted a small trysail on the mizzenmast the boat settled on about 30 degrees to the wind. The wind hardly reached Force 8, it was our jubilee storm, number 10, nasty but short-lived; less than 24 hours later the wind changed to the north and we could sail exactly where we wanted: west-southwest.

Again it was nice and sunny, we could take off our splendid oilskins that had been a really good buy. We could not say that about our new "hurricane lantern"; it was blowing nothing close to a hurricane, but the previous night the lantern was constantly going off. Broad reach sailing is most pleasant, we would have been doing very well if not for a short, nasty swell coming from the west, but we did not complain. At about noon a big, four-engine French airplane flew in our direction and dropped very low; it appeared to be at the level of our mainmast, it made three circles around our boat and flew away. Did the French consider us "lost" again? It could be, all the ships in our vicinity, after spotting us, always changed their course and passed near us. We waved to them, smiling broadly and making all the signs that we were safe and happy, which was true, but our smiles were slightly forced; we were terrified that somebody will again try to "rescue" us.

The beginning of Saturday, the seventh of February was not a pleasant morning. The wind had died completely, *Chatka* was rocking on the old swell. At nine in the morning we noticed on the western horizon a black steamship steaming (as steamships tend to do) in our direction. We did not have any doubt that it was a steamer; from her funnel an enormous plume of black smoke was going vertically up into the sky. That was not a good sign, it meant that she was steaming with the wind, the westerly wind, and we could expect that this wind will reach our position. But soon the steamer outran the windy area, and she was near us. We could see the white name on the black hull—*Wisła!* An old ship from the Polish Steamship Company located in Szczecin. They stopped the engine and we were both immovable, next to each other. Without wind we could not maneuver closer to the *Wisła,* but her captain decided to do an exercise in seamanship: the crew neatly launched one of their motorized lifeboats, and in minutes they were alongside *Chatka.* We thought that we would meet some of our friends from the Maritime Academy, but there was nobody who had graduated in our time. The commanding officer had asked do we know our position. I said:

"Yes." With a mischievous smile he asked again:

"What is it?" We had just established our position, I did not even have to look at the chart.

"36 degrees, 31 minutes north and 0 degrees, 45 minutes west." His smile broadened, he took from his pocket a piece of paper and handed it to me; *Wisła's* position was marked there, it differed from ours less than a mile, only because it included the tenths of the minutes of latitude and longitude.

We were pleased with ourselves, they were pleased with us. In their lifeboat they brought us plenty of delicacies, fancy canned food, cold cuts, fresh potatoes. They inquired if we needed anything else and we asked for some antifouling paint. The French painted the repaired part of *Chatka's* bottom with a standard paint and already, after only not quite three weeks, new marine growth was visible. The wind reached us, we were again mobile, there was no reason for them to go back and forth with their lifeboat, so we suggested that they drop a gallon can of paint into the water, and we would retrieve it. Their boatswain did just that, he lowered the paint on a piece of doubled line making sure that it floats, and pulled the line back. With the freshening wind we executed a faultless "man over board" maneuver, their lifeboat was already hoisted. On the signal yard of *Wisła* were three signal flags: PYU—"We wish you a good voyage"; we did not have the signal flags, we shouted "DZIEKUJEMY."[37] *Wisła* used some of her steam for three long blasts on her horn, we dipped our flag. What a pleasure to deal with simple merchant marine sailors! Generally speaking they do not shoot well, but seamanship is not an unknown idea to them.

We were exactly where we wanted to be, half way between Cartagena in Spain and Oran in Algeria, as far from any land as possible. Finally we were in the Western Hemisphere. Long ago, when we were near Beachy Head in the English Channel, when a huge wave had broken over the boat, our longitude was about 0 degrees, 12 minutes east.

We were aiming towards Alboran Island, a small outcrop in the middle of Alboran Sea, actually the eastern approach to the Gibraltar Strait, about 120 miles distant. After our meeting with *Wisła* we had light winds from a southern direction, and it took us three days to reach Alboran Island.[38] We passed it very closely in order to calibrate our old wristwatches. This island is very steep-to, it always reminds me of a first birthday cake; it is round and in the middle it has one candle: the lighthouse.

---

[37] "Thank you."

[38] On the Admiralty charts this island is marked "Alboran I." Capital "I" is often misread as a Roman numeral one, therefore I have often heard sailors calling it "Alboran the First."

The wind was veering towards east, and soon there was no doubt, we had Levanter, an easterly wind not uncommon in the Mediterranean. It is strongest during late winter and early spring months. This is a warm, eastern wind normally reaching just east from Alboran I, becoming strongest in the Strait of Gibraltar then, after losing some strength, it can blow far into the Atlantic. The biggest question is "how far"? The stronger the wind, the farther it reaches into the Atlantic.

On the approach to the Strait of Gibraltar there is a constant easterly current, and the prevailing wind tends to be westerly. Our old chart had notes for the use by the crews of the sailing vessels, as to which bays are suitable for dropping an anchor and waiting for the end of the westerly. The Spanish coast is doted by those recommended places, at a short distance from each other; obviously there was a lot of waiting to be done.

Fortunately the Levanter is a steady wind. When its strength rises it rises gradually, there are practically no squalls imbedded, with the one exception of the Strait of Gibraltar, where constricting shores form a venturi, and where Levanter is reaching its highest strength, the wind tends to be less steady.

This was our big chance to pass the Strait of Gibraltar, to get to the open waters of the Atlantic Ocean. The Levanter reaches its full strength early after it starts, therefore the sooner we could leave Gibraltar behind us, the better were our chances of having this wind with us for a longer time.

We could see Alboran I before dark, just at the time of the evening visit by the French plane, on the tenth of February, but we did not pass the island until well after sunset. Levanter was getting stronger and stronger, but we decided to go va bank, and we did not reduce the sails. Having plenty new, strong lines, we could reinforce the rigging of the masts with extra stays. Soon it was Force 6, the seas became bigger and we started to surf. Our speed over water reached 8 knots, of course just because of the surfing. The Levanter is a very pleasant wind, but it has one unpleasant characteristic: it carries with it a lot of moisture, and because of this, the visibility is very limited. We spotted the famous Rock of Gibraltar at about sunset of the next day, at a distance of four miles. The Lavanter gave the Rock a wispy cap of a cloud, hanging low over its top. A very small correction of our course was required, we turned a little to the south, to follow the direction of the Strait. This change of the course was also beneficial for our speed, earlier we were practically running free.

Our "friendly" French plane visited us, as usual, at about sunset, and we thought that would be it—tomorrow the ocean. It happened not to be the case. Soon after we had the Rock abeam, another airplane appeared, dropped a little lighted buoy on our course, then another plane flying over us dropped a number of very bright flares. It was bright as daylight. On top of everything we were escorted by two men-of-war which had trained their search lights on our humble *Chatka Puchatków;* they probably were not French, because on our signaling that their lights were blinding us, they switched them off immediately.

The wind, as expected, has risen considerably, we were prepared for this eventuality, we dropped the mizzen and exchanged the mainsail for our "red" storm sail. In order to escape the easterly counter current, which is strongest in the axis of the Strait, we moved closer to the African shore. We must have made an error in the calculation of the time of the high water, because at that hour we were supposed to have the westerly tidal current, which would have made the seas less steep. Instead, we wandered into two fields of sizeable tidal rips. This phenomenon appears as an area of very steep, breaking waves. But we could handle this. We were riding the waves unerringly, this sport added to our speed. We passed the last 22 miles of the Strait of Gibraltar in exactly 2 hours, in the first hour at the speed of 10 knots, in the second 12 knots. After two hours of practice I was quite good at "riding the waves." The secret: just in front of the top of the braking wave (already in the foam) the helmsman has to turn the boat about a point to windward, this causes a bigger force to push the boat forward and the ride becomes longer. Soon we started to time the "time of the ride," the longest I have achieved was almost exactly 20 seconds.

During all that time Janusz was taking bearings on numerous lighthouses; there are rocks here and there along the African shore. Everything was done calmly and efficiently. After all, we had behind us Horns Reef, the English Channel, Mistral; one can get used to almost anything, it seems.

11

*Good bye Europe!—Funchal—Madeira wine—Selvagens Islands—La Palma—Climbing the mountain—*Chatka *is beached—Leaving Santa Cruz de la Palma.*

So, FINALLY WE REACHED the Atlantic Ocean, not only that, we have done it in a fashionable manner: in the last 24 hours we have sailed slightly more then 140 miles, that has given us an average speed of 6 knots! Respectable for any thirty-foot sailboat, for a lifeboat it was phenomenal.

We passed close to the lighthouse standing on the Cap Espartel, the westernmost point on the southern shore of the Strait of Gibraltar. Because of darkness we could not see its square yellow tower,[39] but its light was blinking in a familiar fashion: 4 flashes every 20 seconds. On the starboard we could see (though not very well) the light of the lighthouse on the Cap Trafalgar. Yes, no question about it, we were on the Atlantic Ocean. With all that excitement we did not even have

---

[39] This lighthouse has a strange history: it was built in 1865 (fifteen years before the birth of my maternal grandmother); a year earlier, the sultan of Morocco had signed a pact with the United States of America, cosigned by Austria, Belgium, Spain, France, Great Britain, Italy, Netherlands, and Portugal. That pact has stated that a lighthouse will be built on sultan's soil and maintained by the consortium of kings, queens, emperors, and one president. The same 79-foot tower built more than 100 years ago is topped by a much newer light source.

Chatka *in calm weather. Picture taken from* s/s Wisła.

to disrupt our watch pattern. At ten o'clock Janusz took the tiller, I did not go to sleep, instead I cooked a nice dinner (after all, there was some disruption in our routine, Janusz had been too busy with navigational chores to cook). Then, outside of the Strait, Levanter set again to the most welcome Force 5 and I changed the sails (how many times lately?). Of course we did not keep our breathtaking speed as before, but four knots of easy sailing suited us very well.

Then a worry set in on us: could we find the Madeira Island? Levanter was with us, it was great, no tacking, no rain, but also no good visibility. It was a strange weather condition; no fog, not even a mist, but the air was laden with moisture, and we could not see farther than four miles.

While "taking the sun" on the small boat, the greatest problem was the low elevation of the observer above sea level. If the waves were of considerable height, they obscured the line of the horizon. We had to stand on a bench, holding the mast with one hand and trying to handle the sextant with the other, in order to measure how high the sun is above the horizon. The present situation was different; while standing higher, the line of the horizon became fuzzy, and the accuracy of the observation suffered. Fortunately the seas were not too high; standing about 6 feet above sea level, we could see the horizon quite well.[40] As I had mentioned before, the visibility was about 4 miles, for quite a while we did not have anything on our course, for 530 miles almost exactly, which is the distance between Cap Espartel and Porto Santo, the easternmost island of the Madeira Archipelago, dependency to the Portugal.

Between the Strait of Gibraltar and Madeira there is a relatively strong, southerly Canary Current. Considering that our course was close to the west, this current was practically perpendicular to our course. On Porto Santo (or more exactly on the tiny Cima Island) there is a very powerful lighthouse. We expected that its light would penetrate the not very transparent atmosphere, and so we tried to quickly descend to latitude 33 degrees, 10 minutes north, just a few miles north from the position of the lighthouse. We were slightly too careful regarding the current and we reached this latitude as soon as the fourth day of sailing. We had to be careful, just a few miles south of Madeira there are three islets, Ilhas Desertas, forming a practically unbroken narrow chain, more then ten miles long, almost exactly in the north-south direction. Those islands were uninhabited and unlit, presenting to us their windward shores.

I have spent most of the daytime calculating our longitude, not trusting our only one working wristwatch; I was trying to improvise. The time of sunsets and sunrises could be observed very accurately, and by having the exact length of a "day" and "night" and knowing the change of the time of sunsets and

---

[40] The distance to the horizon in nautical miles equals the square root of an eye height in meters multiplied by 2.08; in described case it was 1.41 x 2.08 = 2.9 Nm.

sunrises, we had to deal only with the daily (not compounded) error of the watch. I can tell, with great pleasure, that those efforts paid off. We were supposed to see the Porto Santo light before sunrise of February 16, and that is what happened, the sky had already started to lighten when Janusz spotted Gp. Fl. (3) ev. 15 sec.

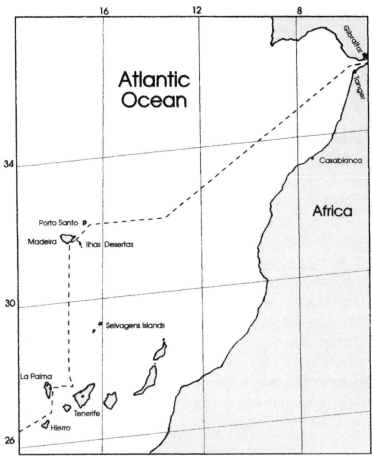

The course of Chatka Puchatków *from the Straits of Gibraltar to the Canary Islands.*

I have to admit that the last two hours before sighting were tense; we should have spotted this light a few hours sooner. We soon knew the reason: fast changing bearings gave us a position less then ten miles from the light; the stated range of that lighthouse is 29 nautical miles. Obviously the moisture laden atmosphere was less transparent than we had thought.

At sunrise the light was gone, and we did not see anything but the surface of the sea. Nevertheless we had our exact position, and after a few more hours we could see Punta de Sao Lorenco, Madeira's easternmost promontory. Visibility was worse than before, and after changing the course towards Funchal we lost sight of the shore again; we were crossing the bay and we were less than three miles from land. After about two hours we could see another cape, another hour of steering close to the shore, and Funchal, the capital and the only harbor of any significance was in sight. Shortly after noon, *Chatka* entered the port, and we were looking for a place for our boat in a very crowded space. It was impossible to reach the quay, we were separated from it by three rows of local fishing boats, we moored alongside one of the boats in the outer row.

Very pleased with ourselves, we erected a spacious tent, using our sails as usual; we put on our "shore" clothes and started towards shore. Before we crossed the first boat, a policeman on the quay stopped us. We did not pay any attention to the small crowd on the shore that had assembled during our preparations, but soon it was apparent that we were expected. The assembly on the shore included the harbormaster, members of the yacht club, immigration officials, newspapermen. A number of people spoke perfect English; there was no problem with communication. The harbormaster, who was sympathetic to us and clearly annoyed with the authorities, explained that because we were from a communist country we were not permitted to leave the boat. I asked if one of us could go to the Post Office to pick up the mail. After a short conference with an immigration official, the answer was "no," but he immediately offered to bring the mail himself. The Post Office was very near, in less than ten minutes he was back, with a very welcomed big package of letters.

We retired to our tent and enjoyed our mail. Besides letters, it contained literally hundreds of newspaper clippings about our trip. It was unbelievable what kind of news and opinions were published. Many editorial cartoons: some making fun of us, some making fun of our critics. To tell the truth we could hardly understand why so many people, who did not have anything to do with the sea, were voicing their totally ridiculous opinions. On the other hand, it was a pleasure to read the articles of experienced sea captains pointing out how valuable our experiments were. It was a real madness, it seems that everything started when our "sinking" near Marseille was reported, then the panicky French authorities, then the French Navy "rescuing" us. In the Polish Communist Party official newspaper high-ranking communists were voicing their idiotic opinions; poets were composing verses about us or our trip. We were amused.

In the meantime the crowd on the shore had increased. People were very hostile to the officials and were trying to show their friendliness towards us. We noticed a small rowboat lingering not far from our *Chatka*. On the shore the crowd became more restless, the policeman became incensed and lunged towards a vocal abuser. This was staged, a few movements of oars and a small rowboat slid next to us, a bottle of madeira wine was deftly put inside our boat. Soon we learned that it was a bottle of an excellent madeira wine.

We read late into the night; in the morning the situation was similar: a friendly crowd, a hostile policeman. After long negotiations an official of the yacht club was allowed to pay us a visit. He brought a basket of local delicacies and the news that his club is trying to influence Lisbon to give us permission to visit the town. During a friendly chat he confirmed that the local sailing community was waiting for us, that they were worried about bad visibility, and that they never expected such a stupid reaction from the local officials.

At least we were allowed to visit Funchal—in the company of two plain clothes policemen. They were not comfortable company. We visited the Post Office, admired white oxen pulling sleighs on the basalt-paved, steep streets, stopped in a small tavern for a glass of the "best madeira wine,"[41] and bought some supplies in a local market. The market in Funchal is an extraordinary place, very clean, and it offers almost everything, including outstanding sausages and an incredible variety of fruit. The climate of Madeira varies (depending on elevation) from temperate to tropical, therefore very many varieties of plants are cultivated there. We bought many things which we were not familiar with, most were delicious, some probably required some special, unknown to us method of preparation and sadly ended up overboard. The fish market was dominated by "peixe espada," a deep-water fish with big teeth, an enormous mouth, and a stretchable stomach.

We left Madeira the same day with mixed feelings. Finding this island with our instruments and in such poor visibility was a feat of navigation. We were welcomed very warmly by members of the local yacht club, and by all the locals, with the notable exception of the functionaries. There was no reason to linger any more in Funchal.

---

[41] Really it was excellent: very rich, heavily spiced, the consistency of a light oil, but not sweet. Since that time I have tried many madeiras; none has approached the taste of the wine in that tavern.

Our next destination was Santa Cruz de la Palma in the Canaries. Why the Santa Cruz de la Palma? There were a few reasons, all of them good. The trade winds are stronger farther offshore, reason number one; La Palma and Hierro are farther from the African shore than any other island in the Canaries. One could stop in Santa Cruz de Tenerife, but this is a big commercial harbor. Supposedly the beautiful Puerto de la Cruz on the northern shore of Tenerife did not get a good review in the Sailing Directions,[42] and the course from Madeira to Tenerife would take us uncomfortably close to the dangerous Selvagens Islands. Hierro has a small, uncomfortable harbor.[43] On the other hand, Santa Cruz de la Palma has a snug, comfortable little harbor.

Instead of stopping in the nearby Canaries, it was possible to go to the Cape Verde Islands, using one of its ports as the final stop before crossing the Atlantic. Many travelers had done this, the distance of the actual crossing to West Indies being much shorter from the Cape Verde Islands than from the Canaries. Their latitude is almost the same as Martinique's, but again the course would pass too close to the African shore and there could be problems with the trade winds. Besides, while taking an arched course from the Canaries towards the West Indies, the total voyage could be shortened by hundreds of miles. All those arguments we can call a good reason number two.

When plotting the course from Cap Finisterre, the northwestern tip of the Iberian Peninsula towards Cabo Branco, the

---

[42] I had visited this place some other time. It is not much more than a boat harbor; anytime there is any wind from the northerly (prevailing) direction, enormous swell makes it totally unusable.

[43] I had visited this island sometime later as well. At the jetty there is a tap spouting outstanding spring water.

easternmost point in South America[44] (for example when sailing from northern Europe to Rio de Janeiro or Buenos Aires), the shortest route will pass between La Palma and Tenerife. Slightly more than a year before *Chastka's* trip, I was on a ship carrying goods from Baltic ports to Argentina and Brazil. It was a beautiful early afternoon when we were passing close to Santa Cruz de la Palma. The view was of outstanding beauty, and I said that I must visit this place sometime. The officer of the watch answered by more or less Polish equivalent of "Yeah, sure."[45] That was the third and most important reason to visit La Palma.

The distance from Funchal to Santa Cruz de la Palma is short, about two hundred and forty nautical miles. With a favorable current we should have done it in not more than three days. The Levanter was gone, visibility was "unlimited," a light northeasterly wind—one could hardly desire a better condition. On top of everything, the system of atmospheric highs and lows was similar to the one expected in September, a month when northeasterly trade winds are reaching farthest north.

We passed the Desertas Islands, narrow slivers of rock, where only one, Deserta Grande, reaches in one point the breadth of one mile, but its peak is almost 1,500 feet high; soon even the highest mountains of Madeira were behind the horizon. This idyllic sailing did not last long. The next day we had light winds, oscillating from southwest through south to southeast, there was no reason to tack, we simply dropped the sails and waited for a promised northern wind. About 24 hours later it arrived, and we were again steering towards La Palma.

---

[44] As well it is the easternmost point of both Americas (excluding some islands).

[45] Probably the only English expression which shows that a double positive can make a negative.

Unfortunately we did not know how far east or west we had drifted during the day of contrary winds. Two days in a row were cloudy, and we could not take the sun sight during culmination, but our dead reckoning put us on the latitude of Selvagens Islands and we were slightly worried. This tiny archipelago consists of almost circular (about one mile in diameter), steep-to Selvagem Grande, low Selvagem Pequena, and a number of offshore rocks—some barely awash, some with the seas breaking dangerously above them. These islands are uninhabited and no navigational light is located there. In the spring, Selvegem Grande is full of nesting sea birds and Madeira's company (owner of the islands), sends teams of workers to collect the fully grown, but still unable to take wing chicks, kills them and preserves the meat by pickling them in the barrels.[46] During the calm summer months fishermen come to Selvegem Pequena to collect abundant spiny lobsters. It would be interesting to land on those islands, but landing there is very difficult. In our unwieldy boat it would be an unnecessary invitation to danger. We were moving at a good speed, keeping a good lookout, and we were never close enough to see the Selvagens, which was very OK with us. Finally on the 22th of February the sky cleared at noontime and we got an improbable reading: our latitude was only seven miles north of La Palma. It could be that our southern horizon was not true, and if we were directly north of Tenerife that massive island could have distorted the reading. Visibility was not bad, but we did not see that island's highest peak, Volcan de Teide, which is more than 12,000 feet high and during good visibility can be seen for more then sixty miles. Selvagens Islands are only about 80 miles from Tenerife, so it did not

---

[46] Not any more, not long ago Selvagens Islands were declared a "Nature Reserve" and the birds (mostly shearwaters) are left alone.

matter how bad our observation was, we could not have make a mistake of more than seventy miles. One headache was over, we were south of the Selvagens. There was nothing to do but sail south. The Canary Islands are densely populated, visibility was more than ten miles, there were no offshore dangers, and little else to worry about. Slightly to the starboard there was a high cloud, could it be over La Palma? It was not a solid clue, and we kept our course. Our strategy was as follows: let us keep to the south for another day, then, if we see nothing it would mean that we are too far to the west, we shall turn east and we should see La Palma or Hierro. If we were too far to the east, we should spot Tenerife, turn west and reach Santa Cruz de la Palma.

Not long after sunset Janusz spied a light. It was not very strong, our boat was rocking, and it was difficult to determine the light's characteristic. If La Palma was on our starboard it could be a lighthouse on Tenerife; the light shown there has three flashes, intervals between flashes are 4 seconds; duration of the flashes are 1.3 sec. 1.3 sec. .4 sec.[47] (Morse's "g"). If we had passed La Palma then it could be Hierro which is showing a flash every 5 seconds. We came closer to the lighthouse, until we did not have any doubt—it was the northwestern tip of Tenerife; we were on course but Santa Cruz de la Palma was almost exactly west from our position, less than forty miles away. That cloud on the starboard which we saw the previous day was obviously over La Palma. On my morning watch I saw La Palma, and in the early afternoon we dropped an anchor in the beautifully situated port of Santa Cruz de la Palma.

It was Sunday, when often harbor offices are closed, especially in smaller places, and besides, after the unfriendly

---

[47] On average it was one flash every 5 seconds.

receptions by the authorities in Madeira we were prepared for something similar. Because we had planned that La Palma would be our last port of call before the long trip to Martinique, we wanted to have a good rest. We therefore decided that it did not matter what might happen, we would take it in stride.

We thought that Funchal would be a good place to haul the boat out and paint the bottom, but of course it was impossible. From the place where we were anchored in Santa Cruz de la Palma, we could see the harbor shallows towards the shore forming a quiet pebbled beach, with a number of small fishing boats beached there. That would be a good place to clean and paint *Chatka's* bottom.

A row boat carrying the employee of the Harbormaster Office came to us. We were informed, as we had expected, that most probably we would have to wait until tomorrow, Monday, to complete the formalities. We did not expect that the oarsman had another task to complete: he ceremoniously presented us with a basket of tasty goodies which included a bottle of local wine. Before leaving Madeira we bought (for exactly one dollar) a gallon (imperial) of madeira wine. No problem, we could wait until tomorrow in comfort. We barely managed to make a dent in La Palma's offerings, when the same person, in the same boat, came back and said that all this waiting for tomorrow was a mistake, quite the contrary, officials are ready for us on the shore. That was true, the harbormaster and some local sailors were expecting us, and that was the reason for the speedy delivery of the gift basket and mustering the immigration officers.

The immigration officers, as one could expect of immigration officers, were at first trying to be very official, but soon they pleasantly joined in welcoming us, as yet the unknown friends, with friendly smiles. Then there was a party, a giant crowded party, lasting late into the night; everyone was cheering, eating, and drinking. We also took part in eating and drinking, even though we had to tell our story many times; it was something like the dinners in the French Admiralty in Algiers, but much more spontaneous and much more crowded. When one small restaurant was cleared of its supplies, we moved to another, then to another. Finally it was time to go "home" small rowboat was given to us for the time of our stay. I rowed it to the *Chatka,* then Janusz decided to take a cooling swim around the boat, while I rowed one victory lap around the harbor. Soon we were hard asleep.

Besides sailing and the sea, Janusz was crazy about two other things: one, benign enough, was an interest in books. It was so serious that during his years in the Maritime Academy he became a volunteer librarian. The second was a desire to climb high places. If you remember, in Christianso we climbed the lighthouse, in Paris we climbed the Eiffel Tower, in other places he climbed various things alone. La Palma has a big mountain, the remainder of an ancient volcano, very tall, almost 8,000 feet above sea level and only about four and a half miles from Santa Cruz. Its crater is enormous, more than six miles in a diameter and about five and a half thousand feet deep.[48] Our chart, issued by British Admiralty, showed that a river emptying near Santa Cruz starts near the top of a crater. It appeared to us, total greenhorns in the department of mountain climbing that it was an easy walk: we should simply follow the bed of the river, and after two hours or so, we should reach

---

[48] It supposed to be the deepest crater in the world. Opinions vary if it was created by an enormous eruption that threw out all the material to create a crater, or that prolonged activity created a void below the volcano into which the volcano subsided, creating the present day caldera. Of course, scientists advocating one or the other mechanism, have solid proof documenting their views.

the rim of the crater. That assumption led to perhaps the most dangerous adventure of our endeavor.

The start of the trip was easy; we were walking on the bank of not a very big river, a stream would be a more proper description. Then there was a waterfall, not a big waterfall, it was easy to bypass it, by climbing to the left, then returning right to the stream, already above the waterfall. Then there was another waterfall, bigger, we could manage to bypass it too. We did this maneuvering a few more times, a few more waterfalls. Then there was a big, really big waterfall, many hundreds of feet tall. We employed our old and so far, proven technique. We were climbing higher and higher, the mountain was really steep, soft volcanic rocks were weathered and crumbled easily. We separated a little bit, we could not follow each other, small avalanches of loose rock released by one climber were cascading on the other. Finally I lost my grip and started sliding down on an almost perpendicular slope. A small bush took root in that rubble, and was growing— fortunately for me, on my speedy way down. The place where I stopped on that bush was on the verge of an overhang, there was a void below me, for more than a hundred feet. Scared to move, I heard shouts. Two locals had noticed us, and seeing my perilous position, started to guide me to a safer place. It took many "izquierda!," "derecha!," "arriba!," and "abajo!"[49] to guide me down. Janusz was in a little better starting position, so it took less time to guide him.

It was a great pleasure to be on level ground again. Our guides seemed to be more scared than we were; they probably realized the degree of danger better than we did. We were

---

[49] Left!, right!, up!, down!

really lucky that they were there. They were miners who had just left a mine for lunch and were alerted to our problems when they heard cascades of stones falling down the slope. We had not heard of any mining activity on La Palma. After we expressed our thanks for their rescue operation, we expressed our surprise about the presence of miners. They showed us their "mine"; it was actually a tunnel from which a sizeable amount of water was flowing out. That was what they were after—they were mining water! Basically it can be said that the La Palma is built of volcanic ash, which is sometimes consolidated into tuffaceous rocks; sometimes there are other volcanic or metaphoric rocks, but basically it is a pile of volcanic ash. If there is rain (or condensation from the clouds), water will percolate down that pile of ash, and it will finally be lost in the ocean without ever reaching the surface. If a tunnel were dug into the mountain, its wall would be wet, water would be dripping. It could then be collected into a watertight trough and sent down the hill where it could be used—for example for irrigation. The problem is that when the wall of the tunnel dries out, the dripping stops. Remedy: dig the tunnel farther into the mountain where its wall will be moist and dripping. The miners showed us the tunnel; in that time it was 113.5 meters long. They were paid to increase its length 20 centimeters every working day; tomorrow it would be 113.7 meters long. The tunnel, more properly it should be called the gallery, is laid in such a way that it is slightly inclined upward, which causes the water to run down towards the opening. On the floor a small-gauge railway was laid. It is easy to push the tiny cars up when they are empty, when they are full and heavy they roll outside by themselves.

We were very grateful for the miners' help in climbing down the mountain but they considered us their guests and insisted that we partake in their lunch. Of course we did not want to offend them by refusing their invitation; courtesies aside, the lunch was delicious: Spanish sausage, "chorizo," spicy with garlic and lots of paprika, home baked bread, and red wine.

It was easy to walk down, we simply followed the course of "lavada," an artificial brook created by the miners and encased in concrete; it was watering fields and banana groves near Santa Cruz. The miners wanted to be sure that we did not try to reach the summit the same way, they assured us that this route would not lead there. Their concern was needless, when we saw the sea again we would have ran to shore had we not been so tired.

In Santa Cruz there are decent size tides, sometimes more than six feet. We moved *Chatka* aground at the head of the harbor in order to be able to easily float her again; we did it soon after high water, which was conveniently in the early morning. When the water went out, our boat was lying on the port side; it took no more than an hour to scrape and paint the starboard bottom. With the help of a few local fishermen, we tilted the boat on the other side and scraped and painted the port side of the bottom. *Chatka's* draught was less than two feet; the job was finished long ago before the next high water, already after dark.

We really liked Santa Cruz de la Palma. Nobody was asking for an interview, nobody was taking pictures of us, but everyone was welcoming us with a friendly smile, every passerby was greeting us with "buenas dias." Sometime ago, in the seventeenth century it was the most important city in the Canaries; it was the center of transshipment of goods between Spanish America and Europe. Now it is a small city that incorporates very nicely its "old town" and the more modern additions.

We did not get any letters from Poland and it was difficult to get a telephone connection; we sent a telegram to our friends to inform them that we had reached the Canaries safely, and we gave them the nearby Harbormaster's Office telephone number. We also telegraphed that in two days we would be leaving towards our next planed stop: Martinique in the French Antilles.

We needed some kerosene for our primus, but there was a problem how to explain what "kerosene" means. In Spanish speaking countries there is a lot of confusion about the names of petroleum products. Kerosene could be "querosina" or "petroleo." Gasoline could carry the British name petrol, or "benzina" or "gasoleo." I knew the word "petroleo," it so happened that in Santa Cruz gasoline was called simply "petrol." I mixed these two words and bought gasoline to be used as kerosene—it was not a good idea. The smell was not right, but I was assured that I was getting what I had asked for: petroleo, at least it was what I had understood.

Saving all our provisions during the difficult times in France, we had plenty of canned food for the trip across the ocean. The casks in which we kept our water supply were thoroughly washed and filled with good tasting fresh water; we also bought a big bunch of not fully ripened bananas, which should last for at least a week. The most important gift we received in Santa Cruz was a fantastic rest among very friendly people. The countless beefsteaks we had eaten for breakfast, lunch, and dinner chased with the local red wine have prepared us for a long voyage; we knew that for about a month we would not have any fresh meat. Without any doubt the good Spanish cuisine increased our feeling of well being. A local watchmaker repaired our wristwatches. He did a perfect job, even though I do not think he had ever seen an East European watch before.

There was no telephone call from Poland. We sent some letters, said good-by to our new friends, and on the twenty-fifth of February in the afternoon we left this most wonderful old port city.

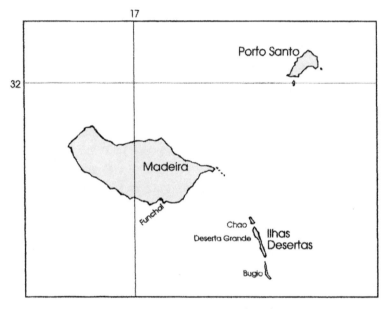

The map of the Archipelago of Madeira.

12

South of La Palma—Flying fish—Sea anchor—Man overboard!—Lost compass—Easy life—Fast sailing—Getting warmer—Mahi-mahi—Tanker Frithied.

ORIGINALLY WE WERE PLANNING to reach the vicinity of Madeira at the end of September. At that time the northern limit of the northeastern trade winds in the Atlantic is farthest north, almost up to Madeira. October is the month when the season of Northern Atlantic's tropical storms is at an end. That would be an ideal time to leisurely cross the ocean and be in West Indies in time for Christmas and New Year celebrations. When we left La Palma it was already the end of February, when the steady trade winds can only be expected far south, at about 19 degrees northern latitude, more than 600 nautical miles from the Canaries.

The distance between La Palma and Hierro is only about 50 miles; it took us a few hours to reach the southern tip of La Palma, Punta Fuencaliente, just in time to see the lighthouse[50] situated there to be switched on. In the morning, island Hierro was in plain view. Hierro in Spanish means "iron." I could not find any sure source of the name of this island, but if indeed it was named "Iron Island" it is a fitting name. Very rugged,

---

[50] Some years after our visit, there was a strong eruption of a volcano in the southern part of the island. The lava flow encased a massive building which forms the base of that lighthouse. A new lighthouse was built nearby. Presently, both towers can be seen standing near each other, only one is showing the light.

with a number of steep peaks looking at it from the sea it appears to be made of rusted iron. We had Hierro in our view the whole first day at sea, and also the next day—the winds were so light that *Chatka* was barely moving. Outside the boat the ocean was full of life. The water was very transparent; we probably could see more then fifty feet deep. A few times the boat entered pools of concentrated plankton; the size of those pools varied from a few hundred to more than a thousand feet in diameter. When putting my hand into such a pool, the sensation was as if it were immersed in jelly, but if a handful of that "jelly" was taken out it was possible to distinguish separate, tiny organisms. For sure, the contents of the smallest pool would be enough to feed a crew of a big lifeboat, but such concentrations of plankton are very rare.

In Algiers we got a harpoon that could be shot from a small gun; it has a pair of rubber hoses which, after being cocked, release and propel a small harpoon with considerable force. This gun is intended to be used by skin divers, but we wanted to use it for shooting from our boat. There were a number of octopuses near the boat, and I was trying to shoot them—many times—unfortunately always missing. Janusz was trying his luck in shooting some small fish, then a big dolphin-fish,[51] also without any results. I know that there are no sea snakes in the Atlantic Ocean, but we saw plenty of undulating creatures, a few feet long, which made a good impersonation of a snake. There were plenty of different kinds of jellyfish, some small, some very large, of different colors—among them "Portuguese man-of-war"[52] a jellyfish-like animal that has an

---

[51] Dolphin-fish, dorado, mahi-mahi, Coryphaena hippuras. I shall stick to the name mahi-mahi, because I do not want to constantly make sure that we are not talking about the dolphin mammals.

[52] Physalia physalis.

air sack, making it buoyant. The sack filled with air—or maybe some other gas—has a crest which acts as a sail; it is a multitude of "polyps" from which hang the tentacles. The float can be twelve inches long, but the tentacles hung down more than 160 feet! I caught one such specimen in the bucket and brought it onboard of *Chatka*. Knowing well about its ability to sting severely, I was very careful, but not careful enough; after thorough examination, when returning it to the water, one very tiny tentacle, so tiny that I did not even notice it, touched my forearm. It caused a red, painful smudge which bothered me for a few hours. Those float-sail combinations capsize ever so often, but right themselves in a matter of seconds. As the sea lore has it, frequent capsizing has caused British sailors to give them this name, Portuguese man-of-war.

Various authors have different opinions about how easy it is to catch fish from a lifeboat. Bombard described his spear, made of a penknife; with this implement he was catching sufficient amounts of mahi-mahi and other fish to keep himself alive for the few months it took him to cross the Atlantic in a rubber dinghy. Others describe the ocean as a watery desert. The truth is, as usual, in the middle. Sometimes the same part of an ocean can be teeming with life, a few months later it can be a "watery desert." Then again there are regions which are not good fishing grounds, period. Nevertheless, a good supply of fishing line, of hooks, some artificial lures should always be a part of an emergency kit on a lifeboat, dinghy, or raft intended to serve as a refuge when the time of "abandon ship" comes. In my opinion the most valuable discovery made by Alain Bombard is the proof that juices squeezed from the fish can be used as substitute for water.

In the warmer regions flying fish can be an important part of the diet. Two nights before reaching the Madeira Island we had our first flying fish of this trip. The next night we had two.

Those fish can soar quite high and for long distances. Most commonly they are collected on a small boat while escaping from something underwater, as they hit the sails and drop inside. There is no question that they fly to the light; often, on large ships, I would find flying fish on the high deck where lights were on for the whole night. The fish that could fly that high (more than forty feet) were the largest. At other times I took part in fishing for flying fish, during a moonless night, from a small dinghy. We would hang a strong lantern on a small pole and, armed with a butterfly net, we would scoop flying fish from the air. During the day their flights often indicate the presence of their greatest enemy: the mahi-mahi. It is a good time to throw overboard a fishing line with anything white on the hook, for example a piece of cloth.

There are plenty of species of flying fish, about forty, but all can be divided into just two kinds: "two-winged" and "four-winged." The two-winged varieties have just their pectoral fins enlarged to form wings; the four-winged have pectoral and pelvic fins enlarged, forming four wings. All of them have the lower lobe of their tail much larger than the upper. Being so close to the surface of the ocean, we could easily observe the whole procedure of taking off. During windy weather the fish would simply accelerate towards the surface and, when in the air they would spread their wings and sail away. When the wind was light and during calm, after clearing the water the fish would spread their wings, but keep tails' lower part in water, and sculling with it furiously they would gain more speed and then fly away. Losing altitude, they could prolong their flight by again inserting their tails in the water, gain speed, and fly farther.

The four-winged varieties are much more agile in the air; they change position of their "front" wings quite quickly. It looks like they are flapping their wings in a bat-like manner and they are able to make sharp turns. But if one can believe what the ichthyologists have to say, these fish can only soar like a glider. Two-wingers fly in a more docile manner, only occasionally making wide turns. In the most important aspect they do not differ at all; at least I could not find a difference how they taste; both are delicious. Another oddity of these fish is the shape of their bodies, their cross-section is almost square, the lower part being flat; this undoubtedly creates an additional lift.

Fishing from the lifeboat can be a good supplement to the stores, but it has to be done in a thoughtful manner. For example, flying fish can be used as bait, of course only if there is fishing equipment on the boat. Captain William Bligh and his crew, during a more than 3,600-mile voyage through tropical waters[53] had fishing lines, but they caught only two mahi-mahi (one managed to jump out of the boat).

We had taken enough food and water to last us through the crossing, even assuming that weather conditions would be far from ideal. Whatever we would catch would be a pleasant addition to our rather monotonous menu. Concerning the weather, we did not do too well; we were in the region of weak, rainy squalls. The sequence of events was as follows: a period of a gentle wind—about Force 2—was followed by a weak squall accompanied by a light steady rain; then the wind would calm down—rain increasing in intensity—then a period of calm, again with very light rain—then back to the previous wind— Force 2 from a southern direction. It was more or less what

---

[53] The captain of *HMS Bounty* was set adrift with another 17 men in a 23-foot long, open boat, by the mutinous crew. His 45-day trip (with 5 stops) from the vicinity of Tonga Islands to Timor was a great feat of navigation. During the trip only one man was lost, killed by the natives in Tonga (four more had died later, one on Timor, the rest on Java Island).

we had during part of the previous leg of our trip, from Funchal to Santa Cruz. This unpleasant weather was with us for three days, finally it had changed to a west by north, and we could hold the desired southwestern course. That day, for the first time, the air temperature was too high for comfort; but both of us agreed that it is much more pleasant than when it is too cold.

The morning of the third of March greeted us with strong, rainy squalls; soon the wind had changed to north, it was fast sailing. During Janusz's watch our mainsail started to wear out around its clew, and before my turn at the tiller I changed the standard mainsail for a storm sail. We did this for the first time since our passage through Gibraltar Straits. The wind freshened to almost Force 6, and during that relatively moderate wind our mast broke, just under the shrouds. It was a new

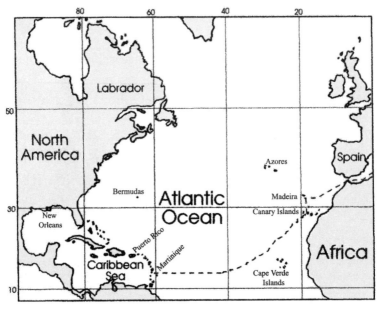

The course of Chatka Puchatków *across the Atlantic Ocean.*

mast made in Algiers, and it had an internal fault in the material; it could be expected that a mast which has lost its shrouds and backstay, would be broken again when pushed by the sail. This did not happen, the parrel with the yard had simply slipped harmlessly down the mast.

In order to steady the boat, which without sails was rocking wildly, we set the sea anchor. On the long, oceanic waves it was holding splendidly, and *Chatka* kept her bows directly towards the wind and the seas. We unstepped the mainmast, or whatever was left of it, and started to work on the rigging. We were trying to do everything as fast as we could; we wanted to use the strong wind from the favorable direction to reach 19-degree northern latitude, where we should find the steady trade winds.

The mast broke about three feet below the top, less than a foot below the shrouds. What was left was a 6-meters pole (less than 20 feet), therefore it would be only 5 meters (about 16.5 feet) above the bench level, where its upper fastening was situated. In order to use its whole length we fastened the fitting for the shrouds to the top of the mast. We had strong pieces of chain which originally were used to secure oarlocks to the boat, together with the shackle we made a ring of it, and set it on the fitting holding the shrouds, forestay and backstay, and we fastened the blocks for the halyards to that chain. It took some gymnastics to stepp the mast when the boat was rocking, but this time there were two of us for this job, nobody was needed at the tiller, so we did it. In a few hours everything was ready, the mast stepped, all the rigging tightened more or less properly: already it was night; we had to do it by feeling rather than by sight.

Wind was increasing and had reached Force 8; not being totally sure of our jury rigging, we decided to carry only the small storm jib, we simply did what we had done during the stormy weather on the shallow seas where the waves were short, or during Mistral when seas were confused. Steering was very difficult, it was dark, we could only occasionally see the ghostly light of fluorescence of the braking waves. The state of the newly rigged mast was constantly on our minds; had we done the repairs right? Would it hold? We still had a lot of territory to cover, but that was not a great worry: we would do it one way or another, we still had a mizzen mast which could be switched in place of the main, we still had the oars, about 4 meters (about 13 feet) which could be used as a jury rig mast, we had plenty of other spars and spare sails. But we wanted to come to the finish in a proper way, not to linger any more than forty days, we were spoiled by our previous successes, we could never do anything wrong, right?

With all this bravado, that evening we did not feel very secure. We were on the ocean; long seas were normally easy to sail on, why was steering so difficult? Before I took the tiller on my watch, I dug deeply into our personal equipment compartment and pulled out one of the safety harnesses presented to me by Peter from the *Hyperion* at the beginning of the trans France trip. I did this for the first time during the whole voyage, I had not worn it during the Mistral or when passing the tide races in the Straits of Gibraltar. Normally, at sea, we slept on the lee bench, cozy in the corner between the bench and the gunwale. This time Janusz made himself a bed in the middle of the boat. He constructed it with oars, spare spears, and sails. From time to time spray was coming into the boat, so we were wearing our oilskins. The wind had increased to Force 9, but the seas were not very high they did not have time yet to increase enough to match the strength of the storm. Taking advantage of a temporary slack in the wind I started to examine the rigging: with a strong waterproof flashlight I checked the sail, it was working fine, then I carefully checked the fittings of the shrouds, one by one. Suddenly a cascade of water covered me; when it passed and I opened my eyes, I saw the white side of our boat, illuminated by my flashlight. I was overboard! My first thoughts were "I really had a good premonition, damn it." I started to pull myself up by the line with which I was attached to *Chatka,* it was not easy, I was wearing long rubber boots, heavy pants, a long jacket down to my knees, and a hat (secured by a chin strap). In a few seconds Janusz was outside the sails and helped me over the gunwale into the boat.

Before that unpleasant happening, we were sailing on the starboard tack. After it we had the wind on the portside, the jib was backing, the boat was drifting. First things first: we put the boat back on the southern course, jibed back to the starboard tack, and started to bail out the boat. The worst thing which had happened was the loss of the steering compass, this time it was not in the bottom of the boat—as had been the case in the English Channel—a wave took it overboard. Lots of things were soaked in salt water, including our sleeping bags. Fortunately most of the spare clothes, charts, and books were locked in waterproof containers. It took many hours to put everything in order.

Again it was cold, for the first time after entering the Atlantic, but this time we knew that in a few hours the temperature would rise; besides, we felt cold only because of the soaking, that was true especially in my case. Again, steering was difficult; the boat was yawing more than ten degrees in both directions. Finally daylight came and we could see the reasons for our trouble. It was the way the long oceanic waves were breaking, when the crest of a particular wave starts curling it moves faster than the non-breaking part of the wave. The comber increases in length, but its curl is no longer parallel to the crest of the wave; in the final moments, it forms a big crescent, its sides are at a considerable angle to the crest. The helmsman has the breaking waves coming from many different directions. If the speed of the boat is very slow, then it will be impossible to take every wave from astern. We decided to hoist a storm mainsail and see how the boat would behave when her speed increase. It was working like a charm, we could see the forming combers and could escape them. During the rest of the storm the boat was running dry. I have to add that this kind of a ride could be very dangerous; if the helmsman is not very experienced in steering during heavy weather that could lead to pitch-poling. If there is a sea room, during a storm when the seas are long and not confused, the safest way is to wait out the storm on the sea anchor.

The storm was holding the whole day, with the darkness its strength had diminished a little, finally the morning of March 5 welcomed us with fine weather, wind NNE, but no trade winds yet. The standard morning cirrostratus was soon gone and the sky was totally cloudless. Again, we could put everything in fine order onboard of *Chatka* and dry all our equipment. Janusz repaired the damaged clew of the mainsail, and it was again possible to carry our full suit of sails; we had time to cook a fine dinner. Since we did not have much to do, we could start to cook various soup concentrates, of which we had plenty. My favorite ox tail soup had disintegrated into a muddy gook, but all the rest held fabulously. The best was pea soup and mushroom soup; the second course was usually something done to the canned meat.

On Saturday, March 7, we entered the trade winds. The difference in the weather was very well marked, the morning stratocumulus fast transformed itself into many well developed vertically cumulus, the wind started to turn more to the east and finally stabilized itself as a northeaster.

We were on an ocean more or less devoid of life, no fish were visible, there were no flying fish during the day, at night none of them were falling into the boat. We could see only a great variety of jellyfish and some mollusks, probably large squid. We were too far from shore to expect octopuses, but I remember that once, when we were sailing in the Mediterranean, more than a hundred miles from any shore, a small octopus fell into the boat.

Finally I knew that "petroleo" from Santa Cruz de la Palma was the same as British petrol, or simple gasoline. When I was cooking breakfast, our primus exploded, burned my face and my right hand. A very, very unpleasant happening, not only that I was in bad shape, but also we did not have any implement to use as a stove. I improvised: using marlinespike, I punched a number of holes in a low tin can which when filled with the fuel (mixture of La Palma petrol and some of our old kerosene) and lit gave a cloud of black smoke and some heat, sufficient to cook or fry our food, to boil water for tea or coffee.

Lack of the steering compass was not a problem. During the day we could steer very accurately using the direction of the waves, from time to time verifying the course on our standard compass, mounted on the bench. During the night, for the first few hours after sunset, Venus was in a proper position to give us good direction, later it was the constellation of Orion, then Ariadne's Wreath. Almost all nights were cloudless, but the night after the primus' explosion Orion was obscured, and I had to steer with my right injured hand, keeping the Polar Star on the starboard beams. During one moment of inattention, the tiller hit the top of my hand, tearing off a big blister. It looked worse than it really was, and after applying pulverized streptomycin, it healed in a few short days.

Chatka Puchatków was rigged as a typical lifeboat, carrying lug sails. It had obvious advantages; most importantly the rig was very simple, even inexperienced sailors could cope with the task of setting sail. Parrel is already around the mast, the mainsail is bent to the yard. It does not have a boom, which can be injurious to the crew. When the mast is stepped, it is enough to place the yard's eyelet on the parrel's hook, fasten the mainsail's tack to the mast, run its sheet to the stern; the sail is then ready to be hoisted. The mainsail has only one halyard (gaff rigging has two), it does not have hoops, its square shape allows the use of a shorter mast.[54]

When we sailed farther south, the trade wind started to blow almost exactly from the east. We were running downwind, and in that condition we would have to use some spar to keep the clew of the mainsail far outside the boat. We could not have done this before, when the wind was variable, or when we had to be ready for maneuvers. The trade wind did not change for days and days; we were able to slightly modify our sail plan; by moving the tack of the mainsail to the front of the mast and to starboard, we had in effect a square sail rig,[55] best for the boat on the course before the wind.

During this part of the trip, Janusz and I were "seeing" each other just a few hours a day. The luxury of sleeping as long as we wanted was a novelty for some days. We were sleeping for up to ten hours! The watches were very easy, easy sailing, easy steering, we kept 12 hours on, 12 hours off, noon to midnight. We spent two hours on cooking, "shooting" the sun, maintenance, some repair of the sails, inspection of the rigging.

---

[54] Shorter mast makes it easier to stepp, keeps the center of effort (center of the sail area) low, this in turn makes the boat more stable.
[55] Some call it a "dipping lug."

Soon the novelty of long sleep wore off. Our neglected library, well protected in a waterproof tank near the helmsman was again in favor. We were so used to steering by the "feel" of the waves, that during the day the "man on the watch" could easily keep the course while reading a book. We were both great fans of Joseph Conrad. *Line of Shadow, Lord Jim, Golden Arrow* were reread for the umpteenth time. The same applied to the stories about a fellow whose name we shared: Puchatek.[56] I think it is obvious that we were both nuts about the sea. On *Chatka* we had a good collection of professional litera-ture, which was in great demand. Of course we also had books about other sailors making small boat passages: Slocum, Voss, Gerbault.

During the night of tenth and eleventh of March, two flying fish fell into the boat—one very small, unfortunately discov-ered too late to be thrown live back to sea, the second, quite big, was our first fresh food after we finished our bananas from the Canaries.

During the day part of my watch the sky lost its typical trade wind appearance. Scared that we were losing the trade winds, I steered the course as much to the south as our new rig permitted. It worked, the next day we regained the glori-ous trade wind clouds. Reading the books by Slocum or Voss, we gained some valuable advice on how to proceed; by read-ing Gerbault we found that if we did exactly the opposite of what he was doing, we were fine. In my later days, I had a friend, a physician who when in doubt sent a patient to one of his colleagues for a second opinion, and then did exactly the opposite of what his colleague had recommended.

---

[56] Winnie-the-Pooh, in Polish, just reminding.

These kinds of people[57] are very useful, as long as it is understood that their opinions (usually very forcefully stated) must be taken in the negative.

Our methods of astronavigation were simple: in the morning, noting the time of sunrise (normally the time of the appearance of the upper part of the sun's disc was easier to "catch") gave us the longitude, at noon the altitude of the sun above the horizon gave us the exact latitude. At sunset the same observation as in the morning, in reverse, noting the time when the sun disappeared beyond the horizon gave us a longitude and the amount of miles we had sailed in the day just past. From time to time we made standard observations of the sun, calculating our position; those were in approximate agreement with longitudes taken during sunset and sunrise. Of course we kept dead reckoning, getting our speed over water by using a chip log,[58] all three methods were close enough to keep us satisfied that we knew where we were. The most important fact was that we knew our latitude with great accuracy. If we made an error in calculating the longitude, it would mean that we would reach Martinique slightly sooner, or slightly later. Two or three days in either direction would not count for much, after almost nine months on the boat.

During the twelfth of March we had excellent conditions for calculating our position; it was 18 degrees, 15 minutes north

---

[57] Like the colleague of my friend or Gerbault.

[58] Simple device consisting of a weighted piece of wood (chip) floating vertically, attached to a string with knots. After the chip was thrown overboard, the number of knots passing out at the given time was an indication of how fast the ship was sailing. It could be constructed in this way that if the ship was sailing at the speed of one nautical mile per hour, one length of the string between knots would pass between the fingers of an observer; double length would indicate that the ship was going twice as fast and so on. This is the genesis of the unit of speed, a "knot": one nautical mile per hour.

and 35 degrees, 00 minutes west. It meant that the distance to Martinique was almost exactly 1,600 nautical miles, as an albatross flies, a hundred or two hundred more on our curved course. The average speed from the Canary Islands was 93 nautical miles per day. Taking into account the few days of calm weather, this was very respectable. Because we were thoroughly rested, long periods of uninterrupted sleep were not as tempting as before, and we decided to keep 6 hour watches, changing at 6 and 12 AM and PM.

Our main compass did not have a phosphorescent card, so when checking the course during the night we had to use a flashlight. Its light was blinding, it took a good few minutes for our eyes to accommodate again to the darkness. Since I had plenty of time I constructed a small oil lamp and attached it to the main compass; it gave just enough light to enable us to read the compass and it was not blinding. Probably this was a coincidence, but the first night when it was lit, I was startled, somebody, in the middle of the ocean was patting my shoulder! It was not somebody, it was something, more exactly a big flying fish. During breakfast (fried flying fish), when I was telling Janusz how the fish was caught, his comment was that I should be grateful it was not a swordfish.

Whenever Janusz looked at me, he could not restrain himself from smiling. Soon he began to convince me that I should get a good portrait of myself in the middle of our trip. That made me suspicious, and I tried to find a mirror to see what made him so jolly. All surfaces of the cans were already matted, water surface in a dish was not steady enough, finally I remembered that there was a mirror in the sextant! A quick look and the mystery was gone: my face was blackened from the fire of our stove (my face was burned by the explosion of the primus; and I had not washed it for a few days); my eyebrows were singed, my mustache likewise, so too were my eyelashes and some of my hair. It was our fifteenth day from La Palma, and I hoped that it would take at least fifteen days more before we would reach Fort de France, Martinique's harbor. During that time I should regain my usual appearance.

The temperature of the air was getting so high that it became uncomfortable, but the good trade wind was blowing, not only was it pushing us to the west, towards West Indies, but it also had a pleasant cooling effect during the heat of the day. Most of the time the sky was full of small cumulus, but sometimes it was replaced by stratocumulus or fractocumulus, normally forming at the end of the day and accompanied by light rains. Those rains were almost always forerun by a squall, always at the edge of the cloud.

Two hours after culmination, the sky was getting clearer and clearer, and about one hour before sunset it was totally cloudless. Then again some clouds were forming, the first half of the night had few clouds, cirrus, and it was possible to steer by the stars. At about three in the morning cirrus were replaced by cumulus, which could change into fractocumulus or stratocumulus. Nights were very damp, the air was saturated with the moisture, and those six hours of the watch in darkness could be chilly, even though the temperature was hovering around 80 degrees Fahrenheit. It may sound ridiculous, but sometimes we would wear our oilskin jackets.

The squalls were never stronger than Force 6, sometime the trades calmed down to Force 2, but generally their strength was between Force 3 and 5. It was easy to forecast: if the trades deviated from their average strength, then in the near future they will change more or less the same degree in the other direction; it could be said that they were trying to keep their set average.

According to all the predictions we were safe from tropical storms at that time and at that latitude of the Atlantic Ocean, but on March 16 the cirrus clouds appeared to radiate from one distant point. This was typical for a forming tropical disturbance, but a few hours later the sky regained its normal trade wind look.

The next night, during my watch, a big flying fish fell into the bows of *Chatka*. It landed on the bench, and I was afraid that it would jump overboard. I ran forward, jumping from thwart to thwart, I grabbed the fish (it was really big), but when running back, I slipped on the last thwart and landed with my face on the lit, jury rigged oil lamp. This did not help my not fully healed face; the poor lamp was devastated. The sound effect was impressive; Janusz's first idea was that the mast had broken again. When he untangled himself from the sails, and in the light of flaming spilled oil, he saw the moving tiller but no helmsman, he thought that I was again thrown overboard. The reality was different; I was at the bottom of the boat, with the fish in my hands.

One night, not many days before the full moon, the trades were blowing at their peak. The dark clouds were racing above our heads, Janusz did not feel like going to sleep, so he kept me company during the night part of my watch. Suddenly there was a sound like heavy rain, hundreds and hundreds of flying fish were taking off, sailing, dropping back into the ocean. We could see this activity very well by the bright light of the moon. Soon the flying fish were gone; they were replaced by tuna fish and mahi-mahi. Those fish did not behave in the usual fashion either, instead of following the flying fish, they were jumping high above the water. They were big fish, and when they were splashing back, it sounded like lots of big logs being thrown into the water. Then there

Taking first bearings on Martinique.

was a period of quiet, not long, but well pronounced. It ended with heavy breathing, on both sides of our boat. It was a pod of killer whales,[59] six or seven animals, every one about the size of *Chatka*. They kept with us for a while, one was very close to the starboard. Janusz, we can assume on not a very smart impulse, threw an empty bottle at it; he did not score a hit, fortunately. If this mass of muscle decided to attack us it would probably have been the end of our expedition.

The appearance of some land-based sea birds, for example the frigate birds, could herald the proximity of land. Learned ornithologists say that the magnificent frigate birds[60] do not fly outside the sight of land. Assuming unlimited visibility, and the fact that they fly 300 feet high (when trying to locate the

---

[59] Grampus, Orcinus orca.
[60] Fregatidae magnificens.

prey, they really fly very high), then in the vicinity of Martinique they would not fly farther than about 100 miles from this island.

We were sailing, helped by the equatorial current, about 100 miles per 24 hours. But we could see those birds a few days before landfall; it is known, that frigate birds can stay on the wing for a few days, maybe their range is much larger. For most of the day they were soaring high, appearing like a dark dot in the sky, but when the school of mahi-mahi found a congregation of flying fish and started to chase them, the frigate birds immediately became part of the action. When flying fish were in the air, the mahi-mahi were swimming underneath these fish, waiting for it to be back in the water. If a frigate bird would spot this race, it would crash dive for the fish, the fish would then try to take evasive action; the mahi-mahi would always stay under the fish. We had seen hundreds of these kinds of hunts, and the frigate bird always was a winner.

The frigate bird never dives into the water; it never even sits on the water. In order to keep the feathers of its long wings dry, it makes incredible aerial acrobatics. In reality it looks like an aerial clown, it seems that at any moment it will crash, but we never saw this happen.

A day or two after an encounter with the orcas, I speared a big mahi-mahi with our rubber tube-powered harpoon. A school of mahi-mahis was following our boat for a while; I aimed for the smallest one—after all how much fish can two not so hungry sailors eat? I scored a perfect shot: right through the gills. The fish was dead before I reeled it in. We fried it, we made fish soup, it lasted for almost three days; it was delicious. Janusz and I prized ourselves on being good seafood cooks, this time we did not have any sophisticated cooking facilities, but the raw material was just right, very fresh.

The last ships we saw were around Hierro, a few days after leaving Santa Cruz de la Palma. Then, for four weeks we did not meet or see any single boat or ship. It was fine with us, we remembered the encounters at the English Channel, in the North Sea, in the Mediterranean. To tell the truth we planned our cross Atlantic route as far as possible from areas frequented by ships plying commerce. But then, on the thirtieth of March we saw a tanker, her crew saw us as well, they came closer, stopped their engines. It was a nice day, we could communicate by voice without any problem. We did not even confirm our position, we did not want to influence our actions with any outside information. For a lifeboat an encounter with a ship meant the end of a voyage. We have had enough of water, enough of food. I am sure that the friendly crew of the Swedish tanker *Frithied* (because that was the ship commanded by the captain who was kind enough to spend some time near us) would have given us supplies if requested. But we only asked that they radio our position to Poland, which they did, as we learned later.

Our calculations showed that we should see Martinique's lighthouse in the early morning hours of the 31st of March. On the evening of the day when we met the tanker *Frithied,* Monday, I settled down to make some notes concerning the last 24 hours. As my "diary," I was using a large calendar, two pages per week. I turned the next page, for the new week, and with a surprise I found that Monday's date was marked red, same as Sunday! It did not take a lot of detective work to find out why, it was the second day of Easter.[61] I told Janusz about my discovery: yesterday was Easter Sunday, and we

---

[61] In Catholic Poland Easter was celebrated for two days, Easter Sunday and Monday. Good Friday was not a holiday.

did not celebrate it in any manner. It was easy to see that the big mahi-mahi was caught in the morning of Good Friday, unknowingly we were eating fish that day, as well as the next day, nothing but fish, because we were afraid it would spoil.

On the 31st, after midnight, it was my watch. When you are trying to see light appear on the horizon, if you look hard enough, after a while you will see it, it does not matter whether it is there or not. Aware of this I did not look hard toward the west, just a casual glance. Then, once, I thought I saw a light. I decided that it was a good time to have a glass of warm milk. Our stove, a kerosene-gasoline mixture bonfire, was so bright that there was no way I could see any light on the horizon. I extinguished the fire, mixed powdered milk with warm water, drank it slowly, letting my vision accommodate again to the darkness. I then allowed myself to have a peek under the mainsail. There was no question—on the course, I could plainly see, it was the light of the lighthouse on Cap Caravelle of Martinique. For the first time in weeks I changed the arrangement of our sails to a standard lug rig. It was simple—I moved the tack of the mainsail into its normal place. I jibed in order to change to the port tack, then changed course to the southwest in order to clear the southern tip of Martinique. Sunrise was coming, and when I raised Janusz for his watch, the green, splendid Martinique was in plain view.

13

Approaching Martinique—Fort de France—Club Nautique—Janusz sails to France—Preparations for departure.

TIRED AFTER MY NIGHT WATCH; I slept quite well for a few hours, then I woke up and started to admire the scenery: deep blue ocean, green Martinique, our boat sailing full reach. A fresh wind was blowing, we were sailing fast. Before noon we rounded Hell's Point,[62] the southernmost tip of the island. It did not look too hellish, but with the little Ilet Cabrits, lying close offshore, it was possible to imagine that in certain conditions this could be a dangerous place.

We were sailing on the Caribbean Sea, this time very smooth, sheltered by Martinique. Since we were unable to resist a close visit to the famous Diamond Rock, we sailed so close that it took the wind out of our sails, and we drifted so near to the rock, that we could touch it. Before sunset we were next to Cap Salomon marking an entrance to the Bay of Fort de France; after reaching this position we were supposed to turn towards the east, into the bay. The wind had become very light, and we could not make any headway in the desired direction; in the morning we could not make any headway either; a month of sailing with the wind had given our cotton sails big bellies, and we could not coach the boat to sail even in close

---

[62] Pointe d'Enfer.

reach. It took a whole day of trimming the sails, wetting them, playing with the halyards and sheets, to get any effect, and, finally, in the wee hours of April the second, we moored at the little pier of the Club Nautique, the local yacht club.

Then the fun part started. After the boat was safely moored, we both spotted a tap, more or less at the same time, most probably a fresh water tap, at the end of the pier. We raced for it, I do not remember who was first, but both of us had a long drink. On our boat there were a lot of gallons of tepid water in wooden casks,[63] its taste could not compare to the taste of water, fresh from mountain springs. It was possible that this was not water from mountain springs; maybe it was plain city water but it tasted great. This was not the end of the fun; a boatswain of the club, together with his numerous family members, ran from his humble quarters towards the pier. The day before there was an earthquake; people thought this was another one. Soon both parties were relieved, there was no earthquake, a madly running bunch of natives was not about to attack us. In a matter of minutes we were on friendly terms; this was a good development, because we were to be the guests of the Club Nautique for a whole month.

After a short sleep we started celebrating, there were bars everywhere, and the natives did not shun a good rum drink in the morning. We decided to follow their example. Their "planters' punch"[64] was treacherous, it tasted like lemonade, but it had a heavy punch. We did not expect that we would be expected in that faraway place. We were, but when we were discovered, the amount of planters' punches made our French totally incoherent; to tell the truth our French, punches or no

---

[63] At the present time, water is kept in plastic containers. It has a plastic taste.
[64] ½ white rum, ¼ cane syrup, ¼ lime juice.

punches, would not be easily understood by anyone. We were placed in a swanky hotel, where we were bitten by some local insects, and in the early morning we returned to *Chatka*— difficult to imagine, but much more comfortable than the swanky, insect-ridden hotel.

Dar Pomorza had visited Fort de France not long before the Second World War. Many of her officers, now captains: Meissner, Borchardt, Jurkiewicz, instructed us to contact Dr. Paul l'Odeon, the first owner of the first sailing yacht in Martinique. He was also the first civilian surgeon on the island. When *Dar Pomorza* visited Martinique, her crew was treated to a gala dinner; the menu included a lobster salad. Lobster meat is not known to keep well in the tropics; the native's name for lobster is "sea louse." Well, whatever it was, the shore party was food-poisoned by the lobster salad, and Dr. l'Odeon took care of the sick members of the crew of the *Dar Pomorza*. Then one of the sailors developed appendicitis. Who was the surgeon to fix the sailor? Dr. l'Odeon, of course. However he was not the first person to visit *Chatka* the next morning, it was Dr. Sonia Clitandre, a Polish physician, the widow of the first radiologist on the island.[65] Dr. l'Odeon visited us very soon after that. He wanted to have dinner with us in his house in Sainte Anne, not far from Fort de France.[66] We did not know where Sainte Anne was, so I pulled out our chart of Martinique; remember, we had some problems finding this chart in Poland? Dr. l'Odeon showed us on this chart where Sainte Anne was, but he also noticed a big, round stamp "Statek Szkolny *Dar Pomorza*."[67] And that was that, he had to have that chart, and he got it, without a fight.

---

[65] He died of radiation sickness.
[66] Nothing is far in Martinique.
[67] "Training ship Dar Pomorza."

When, a few days later, we attended the dinner at the house of Dr. l'Odeon, previously our chart of Martinique was framed and hung on the living room wall. It was an old chart, issued by the British Admiralty. Maybe U.S. charts carry more information, maybe they are easier to use, but for sure the British charts are prettier. The dinner itself was fantastic, the main dish was a big fish prepared in a local way. The fish was a big jack, but I have prepared many other fish in that same way: our groupers and snappers, wrasses and mackerels. In Chile I have used congrio colorado, an eel-like fish of the cod family; the recipe seems to work well with any kind of fish, with the exception of salmons and flounders.[68]

Martinique was supposed to be the final port of our trip, but after *Chatka Puchatków* had suddenly become famous, the possibility of bringing her to Poland was entertained. When in the Canary Islands, we had proposed that we would sail to New Orleans, nearest to Martinique, regular port of call of Polish ships. The distance Fort de France-New Orleans, about 1,500 nautical miles of favorable currents and winds, could be easily covered within a month of leisurely sailing, stopping here and there on the way. Unfortunately Janusz's health deteriorated; his strange arthritis started to bother him again, and I could understand very well that he was scared of getting a severe attack of it somewhere on the way.

---

[68] A whole fish gutted and scaled, gills removed, is placed in a baking dish. Slices of lime (lemon), onion and sweet paprika are placed inside the fish. Slices of onion covered by the slices of lime topped by a pat of butter are placed on the surface of the fish, generously spiced with ground black pepper. Milk is poured into the pan, ½ of the thickness of the fish deep. Bake for about 20 min. in 300 degree F oven, or until the residue of milk will reach the consistency of a thick cream. Typically it is eaten with tiny slices of a very hot raw paprika.

Communication with Poland was always difficult, but we developed a system: I would send a very short telegram to Staszek Mioduszewski, giving him the telephone number where he could reach us. We made our base in the yacht club cafeteria/meeting room, spending long hours waiting for the telephone connections, fortifying ourselves with planter's punches. A club member, a stately Mulatto in his forties speaking perfect English, joined me at the table. After acknowledging my liking of rum drinks, he stated that he liked them too, but he warned me about their destructive effect.

"Look at me," he said. "I look much older than my age. How old do you think I am?"

I wanted to humor him, so I added a few years to his apparent age.

"About fifty."

"You must be joking. In few weeks I will be sixty-five."

I promised myself to use this rejuvenating mixture in the future, in proper doses.

Finally a decision had come from Poland: find out how much a passage for two on a French ship to any French harbor in Northern France, will cost, transport of the *Chatka Puchatków* included. La Companie Generale Transatlantique, using also the English name French Line, located very close to the yacht club had a virtual monopoly on ship traffic; I got a quote from them the same day: ticket $130 per person, transport of the boat $160, total $420. This information was immediately transferred to Poland.

The location of the Club Nautique was very noisy, it was close to the commercial harbor and the water there was quite dirty. We were given the use of one of the comfortable wooden dinghies of the Club and moved *Chatka* to the "Flamand's Anchorage" on the lee side of Fort St. Louis. The place was ideal, close to the center of town, not far from the

Club, but quiet, clean, and deserted; we were the sole craft over there for more than two weeks. After two weeks a Belgian yacht arrived, a steel-hulled ketch with a crew of two, a Belgian sailor and his wife.

They were a pleasant couple; we spent a number of evenings with them. He had very bad luck; in the last day of the Second World War, May 8, 1945 he was seriously injured by stray shrapnel; after recovery, which had taken him a long time, he lost interest in Europe and decided to spend his time on the boat. Their boat was very well built; the Belgian sailor had a steady invalid's pension. They traveled slowly, staying in any port, as long as they liked it, not rushing anywhere.

We were waiting for the money and we had plenty of free time. According to the natives, the Vichy sailors stationed there during the Nazi occupation of France destroyed the fish population in the nearby waters; they were fishing with dynamite. Scuba divers from the Club Nautique were bringing in miserable catches, maybe five pounds of small fish after using a few tanks of air. With the additional pressure from the local fishermen, the fish stock was recovering very slowly, if at all. That took care of one of my hobbies: fishing. Fortunately I love rowing and had ample opportunity to spend hours and hours on the dinghy, rowing far inland on the two Fort de France rivers, Madame and Monsieur. I rowed far into the head of Bay of Fort de France where it becomes shallow, transferring itself into a mangrove swamp. Those trips were most interesting; I visited a number of tropical ports, but, very rarely, and only for a short time could I take trips into the wilderness.

From time to time Dr. Clitandre took us in her car inland, showing us interesting places. Martinique is very densely populated, outside of the Fort de France it appears to be one big village. Walking in the bush is supposed to be very dangerous because of cobras. Those poisonous snakes were introduced to Martinique at the time of slavery, to discourage slaves from escaping from the plantations. In later times, in order to kill off the cobras the French introduced the mongoose. The island was already densely populated, and almost every homestead had chickens. Soon the mongoose discovered that it is much easier to catch a chicken for dinner than to fight a cobra. Now Martinique has a plague of cobras and mongoose. Dr. Clitandre has antivenin in her office and treats victims of snakebite many times a year. There are hundreds of physicians on Martinique, there must be a considerable number of cobra victims every year.

Once we were invited to Dr. Clitandre's friend, M. Charles Clement, for dinner at his estate. He was the owner of a sugar-cane plantation and a major distillery in the eastern part of the island. A tour of the facilities was very interesting, the dinner was very good, but what was superb was the after-dinner drink: M. Clement's special white rum. One could expect that a major producer of rum would have something special served at his table. But this was not just something special, it was something extraordinary, never before and never after have I ever had anything close[69] to that white rum in a crystal bottle.

The money was not arriving—nothing new about that—to squeeze anything from the communists was not an easy task. Finally Staszek somehow got access to the office of the prime minister, the princely sum, 420 dollars was approved, but we were still waiting. In the meantime, merchant ships were coming and leaving Fort-de-France. Our base, cafeteria of Club Nautique, was also the preferred place where captains and

---

[69] Even though I have searched, and tried, widely.

officers of the visiting merchant ships would came for pleasant evenings. Most of them, I am almost ready to risk the statement "all of them" knew about our expedition. Quite a few were short of crew, because of sickness (or a heavy love attack), the officers or sailors had to be left in Martinique. Sometimes ships were arriving already short of a few hands. Many times we were assured: no problem I shall sign you on as crew, your boat, no problem, it will take just a small space on the deck. Next morning the situation changed, La Companie Generale Transatlantique always vetoed any kind of arrangement that would include the two of us and *Chatka Puchatków* leaving Fort-de-France on any of the boats chartered by that company. We were surprised, our friends in the yacht club were flabbergasted; finally the truth came out, some official of the La Companie Generale Transatlantique wanted to get our boat (at the fire sale price, naturally) to be used as a fishing craft on the windward side of the island where the fish were not depleted!

The money did not arrive until April 26th. We went to our not-so-friendly CGT to finalize the passage. During those three weeks the price of the passage increased, "slightly": the passage per person was not $130 any more, it was $220, the transport of the boat was no longer $160, it was $456. Somebody really wanted to fish with our boat. There was not much I could do; as I have said before, the CGT has had a virtual monopoly in Martinique. Janusz was in no shape to continue a small boat voyage, I booked a cabin for him on *Fort Douquesne* heading to one of the Canal La Manche ports, which one would be determined later: La Havre, Dieppe or Rouen. Dr. Clitandre and I were on the quay, wishing Janusz a good trip. Dr. Clitandre gave Janusz instructions how to meet her daughter, Danielle, who at that time was studying in Paris. As I learned later, he did meet her.

During our stay in Fort-de-France, we met an officer from the ship *Silver Ocean,* a Pole, Mr. Legeżyński. It just so happened that *Silver Ocean* was again visiting Fort-de France, a few days after Janusz's departure. There was a vacancy for a third officer, I and the boat were assured a berth, until the morning, when it was vetoed once more by the office of the CGT. That was that, there was no way I would leave *Chatka* to the scheming French. To tell the truth, I hated single-handed sailing. For me sailing, in good or bad weather is a pleasure, sometimes the pleasure is more pleasant, sometimes it is less pleasant. To go for a day of comfortable sailing, alone in the boat, I have done it countless times. To sail for a longer time alone is not my idea of fun. Of course I know about Captain Slocum, the extremely experienced captain of the square-riggers, who had sailed his *Spray* alone around the world. He did it leisurely (weather permitting), my greatest regards for him. I do not like to leave the ship without anyone on watch; maybe too many vessels have tried to ram me.[70]

There was not much I could do, I had slightly more than two hundred dollars, I was very well rested, a trip to Dominica, an island north of Martinique, was only fifty miles long. I decided to try my luck in English speaking lands. After one month on the Atlantic and another spent in Fort-de-France, *Chatka's* bottom required another cleaning. During the crossing we had observed strange (for us) crustaceans that were attaching themselves by their long stalks to the boat, at the water line. Their shells, about ¾ of an inch long, were multi-colored, off white, brown, and reddish. When undisturbed, the

---

[70] Only one had succeeded, a motorboat at about 60 knots, in the clear weather (35 footer having three outboards at 225 HP each) had given me a glancing hit. Some injuries, thousands of dollars worth of repairs.

shells were opening, and a lot of feathery organs were waving in the water. After landing in Martinique we learned that those were goose-barnacles, very tasty. The few days which we spent in the polluted water at the Club Nautique were enough to kill those animals, but their stalks were firmly attached and served as a base for all kind of flourishing sea-weeds. At the club I met a family of young sailors living across the bay in Trois-Ilets; they assured me that water there is very clean, and they offered me evenings at the bridge table, a game which I did not have occasion of playing for a long time.

The tides on Martinique are very small; I could not beach the boat as we have done in the Canaries. It was true, the water in Trois-Ilets was crystal clear, I had anchored near a small pretty beach, on sandy bottom, less than a fathom deep.

Preparing the boat for a solitary sail.

Wearing a face mask and using a rice straw brush, I dove and scraped plank after plank. It was not an easy task, broken shells were hurting my hands, I could hold my breath only long enough to clean a small area of the bottom. Multitudes of small crabs, about a tenth of an inch long, having lost their home in the scraped weeds, were settling on me. After fifteen minutes or so, I was covered by those small fellows. I had to climb aboard *Chatka* and dive forcefully, so that the water current would free me of the crabs for a while; another fifteen minutes and I had to repeat the procedure. It took me a day and a half to clean the boat properly.

Some sails required attention, I wanted to have all the sails in good condition; sailing alone I would not have time to repair them during the trip. I filled all the casks with fresh water, bought enough food to last comfortably for two weeks; we had bought a new primus immediately after landing in Fort-de-France. I had a general chart of the Caribbean Sea. If for whatever reason I would not be able to land on Dominica, I could comfortably sail farther, and try to reach Charlotte Amalie on St. Thomas, in the U.S. Virgin Islands. This was my next planned port in case I could not manage to get a passage from Dominica. If I were blown farther west, or wherever, I could comfortably spend a few weeks on the boat, and have plenty of time to reach some other harbor.

It was the final game of bridge with my friends in Trois-Ilets. The game was tough and I bid and won, to everyone's surprise (myself included, my hand was not that good) a grand slam in spades.

14

*Departure from Martinique—Roseau—Looking
for a ship—Mr. Wiński—Mountain chicken—
Dr. Czerwonka—Perils of solitary sailing—Charlotte
Amalie—Tortola—RMS Rhone—Port San Juan.*

I HAD TO RETURN THE WOODEN DINGHY to the Club Nautique, so I sailed across the bay of Fort-de-France and tied *Chatka* to the pier which we had left about a month ago. In the Club I had a few last planters' punches, said good-bye to whoever was present there and returned to the boat. It was already late, the wind had died to a dead calm, and after making last checks I rowed *Chatka* about a mile from the shore, beyond the area used by merchant vessels. It was only about twelve hours of sailing from Fort-de-France to Reseau in Dominica; I did not want to arrive there during nighttime so I had waited until the next day in the afternoon before weighing the anchor. I planned to be near St. Pierre, close to the shore and in the shadow of the volcano Mount Pelee, an hour or two after sunset. During that time I should be totally becalmed, but a weak current would push me northward towards the channel between Martinique and Dominica. Because I was very close to the shore, I was not afraid of bigger ships. I had hoisted my good lantern high above the jib, and left all the sails standing. This arrangement allowed me to have a safe night of good sleep.

Everything went as planned: about sunrise the current pushed me outside the shadow of Mount Pelee, sails started to clatter, I took the rudder and sailed on, very fast; the trades between the islands were about Force 5. I was not sleepy at all, soon the morning light showed me the first glance of Dominica: rosy clouds flowing down the rugged mountains, then blood red was a dominant color, replaced by deep green of the tropical rain forest. Less than an hour after the beginning of the show, the sun was up, and that beautiful, wild island was showing off herself.

Another two hours and *Chatka* was in quiet waters, shielded by Cape St. George, the southern tip of Dominica, on the lee of that island. Another one hour and after passing a few picturesque villages I was near Roseau, the capital of the island.

The waters around Dominica are very deep, and I was hugging the shore, trying to enter without tacking the small area of shallows near the waterfront where I could hope for a safe anchorage. This maneuver was accomplished without a hitch; *Chatka* was anchored less than a hundred yards from the shore. It was Sunday (it seems that I had the luck to arrive on Sunday at most destinations) and soon an official, bent on paying me a visit, was rowed next to my boat, offering to clear the formalities for some extra fee. My reason for visiting Dominica was to find transportation to Europe, of course all offices were closed, I could wait until Monday.

This time the erected tent was not to prevent the crew from being cold; quite the contrary, its duty was to offer shade, its sides were open, allowing a gentle breeze—leftover from the trades—to exercise its cooling effect. It was the third of May, a Polish national holiday.[71] The anchor was holding fast,

---

[71] On that date, in 1791 Polish Sejm (congress) adopted a democratic constitution, second on the planet Earth; America's, adopted by Congress in 1787, was first. (The American Constitution, after being ratified by more than nine states, was declared "in effect" March 1789.)

nearby the lee shore gave me good protection against the waves. I decided to have an official banquet, the whole crew in attendance.

Roseau is built on a very small piece of flat and low land formed by sediments carried by the Reseau River, which bisects this little town of about ten thousand people. Its waterfront, lined with masonry warehouses, appears to be much more prosperous than it is in reality. Because it was Sunday, there was little activity on the shore, it was a quiet afternoon; the evening had brought the usual voices of the tropical forest plus insistent and loud barking, which was shorter than dog's and the sound ended abruptly.

I was awakened early in the morning, the nearby waterfront was bustling with activity. On the quay I could see an agitated gentleman, of short posture, with large binoculars which he was often training on my boat. Soon, the same boat as yesterday, brought an official, and I was granted a pratique. I was offered transportation to the shore with the information that the gentleman with the binoculars was waiting to see me. Shortly I was shaking hands with Mr. Karol Wiński, the Royal Surveyor and eminence grise of the island. According to him, *Chatka* was the first boat under the Polish flag that had visited Dominica. That was very probable, this was the second time that this honor belonged to *Chatka:* the first was on the island La Palma in the Canaries. Because the anchorage was safe and Mr. Wiński had instructed the foreman of the waterfront watchmen to keep an eye on the boat, I could leave her alone. With pleasure, I accepted an invitation to spend a few days I was intending to stay on the island, in Mr. Wiński's comfortable hillside home just outside the capital.

The first ship scheduled to visit Dominica was a British banana boat, due in a few days and due to leave the following Friday. We visited an office of the agent of the shipping line, the owner of that particular banana boat, inquired about the possibility of the passage, for the boat and for myself. The agent had promised to use his influence to help in this endeavor, subject to the approval of the captain of the banana boat and the line's office in London.

I learned that Mr. Wiński was not the only Pole in Dominica, there was an oral surgeon, Dr. Czerwonka, both of them had served as officers in the Polish Army, fighting on the Western

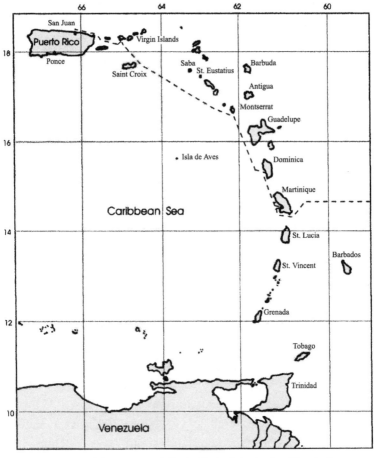

The chart of the course of Chatka Puchatków *in the West Indies.*

Front, and had taken part in the D-day invasion. After Mr. Roosevelt had presented Poland to Uncle Jo,[72] they decided not to return to Poland, and not to live under the communists' rule. They took jobs offered overseas and met each other in Dominica. These men had distinguished themselves during their Army days. Mr. Wiński had some accomplishments in the early days of the war, working with the Polish Underground, and had even earned the death penalty (in absence, of course) from the Nazis. Dr. Czerwonka's physique was the opposite of Mr. Wiński's; he was a big, strong man built like an athlete. As a matter of fact, he was an Olympian; he had competed in the Olympic Games in the javelin throw. He had an important professional achievement as an army surgeon; he had developed a novel surgery for the victims of land mines whose jaws were destroyed; he used part of a rib of an injured person to reconstruct the lower jaw.

That very evening I had a delightful dinner with those two gentlemen. They were pleased to speak with someone who had been in Poland just less than a year ago, and I was enthralled with their war stories. Our drinking habits were similar, even though one of the company preferred Cuba Libre.[73] Dominican rum was not as good as the best rums of Martinique, but on a par with the standard production of lesser Martinique distilleries. In Dominica, planters' punches were served less sweet; in reality that way of preparation was even more agreeable. Soon the main course was served: mountain chicken. In those mountains the chicken must grow big; the bones were thick, the meat more dark, but after all it tasted like chicken, more or less.

---

[72] Not so subtle allusion to the Yalta Conference.
[73] Rum and Coca-Cola, ice and a squeeze of lime.

"How do you like our chicken?" I was asked. It was baked with tasty vegetables, the sauce was pleasant and spiced.

"It does not look much like chicken, but I like it very much all the same."

"Did you hear the barking in the mountains last night?"

"Yes, indeed, I heard it and I was wondering what animal makes that kind of a sound."

"That was the barking of the mountain chickens."

A waiter was summoned and asked to bring the carcass of a dressed mountain chicken. He did what he was asked. On a tray lay a big frog, skinned, but unmistakably it was a frog.[74] I was told that this big, almost two-pound frog lives only on two of the Windward Islands: on Dominica and on the small Montserrat, about one hundred miles farther north.

Mr. Wiński had been offered a choice of work on either of two islands where there were openings for a position of Royal Surveyor (by profession he was a land surveyor), Dominica and St. Lucia, south of Martinique. He could not get much information about either island, but he chose Dominica because it was situated farther north, presumably in a cooler climate. It was a very good choice for a man whose initial task was to make the first detailed map of the island; Dominica does not have any poison snakes, while St. Lucia is famous for the abundance of an aggressive and very poisonous snake, fer-de-lance.[75] These snakes can grow to nine feet in length, they are viviparous, even a tiny newborn (one female in a single episode can have more than 50 sons and daughters) can deliver a bite fatal to a human.

Dominica is a very mountainous island, its highest peak, Mt. Diablotin is 4,745 feet high. This leads to an unusual feature:

---

[74] Leptodactylus fallax.
[75] Bothrops atrox.

both shores are frequented by rainy squalls, normally lasting less than 15 minutes but returning many times in the night and in day hours. The windward shore develops rain due to the trades; the moist air is forced up the mountain, it cools adiabatically and often this process can result in rain. In Dominica, where the antitrades commonly occur in the low altitudes, the same process takes place on the leeward shore as well (which is a windward shore for antitrades). Therefore almost the whole island is covered by lush vegetation, with the exception of its southern and northern tips which are too low to "intercept" the antitrades.

This abundance of rain results in hundreds of streams and rivers, it is taken for a fact, that there are 365 of them, one for every day of the year. When Mr. Wiński had finished mapping the seashore part of the island, the final score was somewhat smaller, but still impressive for such a small island. If those streams, often very turbulent, carve their beds in soft, tuffaceous rock, which is abundant in Dominica, then during a period of heavy rains sometimes they change their course. That leads to the saying, "In Dominica even rivers change beds overnight." Supposedly, at the time of my visit, the marriages were not very stable, and priests in that predominantly Roman Catholic society were not in a hurry to marry couples, demanding something more concrete than a word about their commitment, for example a child or two.

"An expedition" of Mr. Wiński with the Secretary of Public Works and Education was scheduled the next day to inaugurate the planning of a new road connecting an interior village with the already existing network. I was offered to participate in that excursion, an invitation which I joyously accepted; I was very interested in what the interior looked like. Besides the persons mentioned, eight locals came with "cutlasses," something akin to the South American machete—big knives used to clear passages in the bush. In the beginning we climbed a steep path, mostly bordering a precipice, sometimes on the left side, sometimes on the right. We forged a few streams, walked through mountain passes, from time to time meeting people going the other way; some of them were leading burros, having barely room enough to fit on this tiny path. After reaching the targeted village, Mr. Secretary made a speech, graciously mentioning Poland and her brave sons, one of whom had crossed the ocean for the very reason of visiting this very school, and other such nonsense, talking just like politicians everywhere.

After the ceremonies, there was a business part: the locals were showing how, in their opinion, new road should be built (the final route would be determined by Mr. Wiński, naturally). Soon the tiny path became difficult to move through and four natives with cutlasses started to clean the passage. Soon all eight had to be employed in order to keep progressing at a measurable pace. The foreman, who was marching as the rear guard of a working party showed me a spot of tangled bush and said that here was a path to the next village. I acknowledged this information, but to tell the truth, I could see nothing there but a dense growth of "razor grass." Before I could ask why this grass was named that way, I knew, I learned by looking at my skin. The foreman, noticing my interest in everything we saw, pointed to the big hermit crab living in an abandoned shell. This was new to me, I did not know that there were land hermit crabs. I knew about "standard" land crabs, and the minute I mentioned it to the foreman, he had showed me a pair of very big ones. Most probably we had passed plenty of these land crabs, but it was necessary to know how to look for them.

Once when we stopped, while the foreman was telling something, he suddenly looked at me, rolled his eyes and in a loud and ominous tone said "Ahaa?!" I did not feel very sure of what was going on, moreover that foreman in a more loud and more ominous tone, looking straight at me said "Aahaaa?!!" Soon, when he started to roll his yes again, and again went on with his even louder "Aaahaaaa??!!" I pretended to be very busy looking at some interesting tiny plant. In the next second the foreman picked up the previously commenced explanation. It had appeared that he was just... clearing his throat.

We moved forward. The sun was already very hot, and when we left the thicket and started to descend through an open area, the hot stones were burning my lightly-shoed feet. Finally we reached the outskirts of Roseau, next to the house of Mr. Secretary, who invited us for fresh, cool, coconut water, spiced with gin. Almost everyone was tired. The secretary was tired, all the working crew had had enough, I was tired; while Mr. Wiński, about thirty years older than I, was not tired at all. His stamina was legendary in Dominica. Practically everyone on the island knew about him, children were being named (as a given name) Wiński.

That evening we had dinner in Dr. Czerwonka's home, his Scottish wife prepared a Polish dinner, and she did it very well. Dr. Czerwonka apologized that there were not pickled herring on the menu. Pickled herrings? On Dominica? I thought that he was joking. I was wrong, Dr. Czerwonka had a source of pickled herring. The Dutch island of Aruba has a problem with fresh water, while in Dominica, as I have said before, there was plenty of fresh water. Dutch tankers were taking good spring water from Dominica and ferrying it to the Dutch West Indies. In the bay north of Roseau there was a big buoy connected by a pipe to the small reservoir in the mountains. The process of filling the sizeable tanker would take a number of days. If any of the crew had a tooth problem he was transferred to Roseau where the fee for curing a toothache was half a dozen pickled herring (of all the ships visiting Dominica only the Dutch had pickled herring on the menu). It is strange but true, that anybody used to that Baltic and North Sea delicacy, when deprived of it after a while developed an acute craving. I remember that while visiting the South American ports, in expectation of visiting local Poles, stewards on the ships were preparing dishes of herring, previously properly soaked and spiced.

Before the Second World War, the Polish Sea Scout, Władysław (Wladek) Wagner, completed a trip around the world. In July of 1932 he left the Polish port Gdynia in an old motorboat converted into a sailing vessel. Named *Zjawa,* she was in bad shape, but Wagner, together with a few companions (his crew frequently changed) coasted to Dakar, crossed the Atlantic, landed near Belem in Brazil. He again coasted near the northern shore of South America and by way of Trinidad made it to Panama. In Panama he bought a bigger and a more seaworthy unfinished yacht, named her *Zjawa II* and reached Fiji. In Fiji it was discovered that sea worms had destroyed his boat, beyond any possibility of repair. Traveling by a steamer, Wagner returned to South America, and in Guayaquil, Ecuador, built another boat, the sturdy *Zjawa III.* He completed his circumnavigation on this boat and in August 1939 he was in England. A few days later Germany invaded Poland, and that was the end of Wagner's trip. I did not know what had happened to him after the war, but Mr. Wiński had the information that Wagner bought Beef Island, a small isle just to the east of Tortola in the British Virgin Islands. That was an interesting piece of information; if I were to sail to St. Thomas in the U.S. Virgin Islands, I would have a good chance of meeting this famous sailor.

After a few days in Roseau, the expected banana boat arrived. The captain had agreed to take *Chatka* on board, but ship owners in London requested a payment for passage, 225 dollars for me and the boat. It was much less than the fee requested by the French Line in Fort-de-France, but I had only 150 dollars in my pocket, and I did not try to negotiate the fee. To tell the truth I was thrilled by the anticipation of meeting Wagner. Without much ado, I left Dominica on May 8— intended port of destination: Charlotte Amalie in St. Thomas.

Without any doubt, Dominica was the most beautiful place I had ever visited. At that time it was a very friendly island, a member of the West Indies Federation. This federation did not last long, and later on Dominica became an independent nation. During the following years, I visited this island many times. Unfortunately it is not a friendly island anymore. Local politics, rampant crime, racial tensions, resentment against "yachties" do not contribute to a visitor's sense of being

Leaving Roseau.

welcome. On top of everything, hurricane David destroyed most of Dominica's rain forest. High in the mountains, where antitrade winds were blowing and hundreds of fern species—from tiny specimens to huge fern trees—lived in almost constantly present cloud, the rainforest is not the same anymore. After the big trees were gone the climate had changed. Probably it will take nature tens of years to restore the previous splendor.

As I have mentioned, Mr. Wiński's main task was to produce an accurate map of Dominica, and during the time of my visit his work was well advanced. One of the remaining problems was to establish the exact height and location of the highest peak, Mt. Diablotin—it was almost always covered by clouds. After I left Roseau, in order to avoid the squalls falling from the mountains, I moved far offshore, and there it was: I could see the peak of Mt. Diablotin; it was a rare occurrence when cloud was not present. I established my position with great accuracy, then, with the sextant I measured the angle between the shoreline (which was already behind the horizon) and the top of the peak. I later mailed this information to Mr. Wiński.

I weighed my anchor in the midmorning. Both Poles who accompanied me in the small boat which ferried us to *Chatka* stayed with me for a while. The wind that morning was very weak, and it took considerable time to get a stronger breeze. They were rowed to the shore, I was again alone, but provided by Mrs. Czerwonka with a tasty lunch: she had presented me with baked chicken (standard chicken, not of the mountain variety). Before I reached Dominica Passage, a gap between Dominica and Guadelupe, the chicken was finished, the day was gone as well, and I had a night sail through the passage. The night was dark, visibility not very good, a little bit misty, and I was on the lookout for the Les Saintes Islands, a tiny archipelago of tiny, not lit islets lying in the passage. The morning light showed that my worries were baseless; I was a good few miles to the west of Guadelupe which was visible as a big massif rising above the vapors of the calm sea. I was incredibly tired, so tired that I did even not fry a sizeable flying fish, which had landed during the night when the sea was rough between the islands. The wind was light and finicky, I dropped the sails and went to sleep, which again was not easy, the swell was rocking the boat, it was hot, from time to time, small occasional drizzles were making sure that relative humidity was not far from 100%. When I woke up in the late afternoon, the trades had stabilized themselves, they were gaining in strength. Soon it was Force 6, and *Chatka* with a clean bottom, sailing large quartering wind, was moving fast. My idea was to leave the disturbed weather on the lee of the tall, Basse-Terre half of Guadelupe as soon as possible. Trades were not squally, they were blowing evenly, therefore I did not shorten the sails, and the boat was sometimes sailing, sometimes surfing, with the speed approaching eight knots.

Montserrat, a small island in the chain of Leeward Islands was supposed to be on my starboard bows. My calculations, the course I was steering, everything was telling me that I should pass it at a safe distance on my starboard. But after a few hours of such fast sailing, I began to be uneasy; in that part of the Caribbean Sea the currents can be very capricious, changing speed, sometimes direction as well, something was telling me that Montserrat is on my course. I dismissed such fears, and had sailed for another few hours, then I gave up: why worry, it was about four in the morning, I could use a few winks. After dropping the sails, I allowed the boat to drift in the westerly direction, with the more or less northerly current I should move where I wanted, towards the northwest. After dozing on and off for about an hour, I saw a weak light appear in the east, soon it would be dawn. It is a pleasure to observe the birth of a new day, the sky was getting lighter and lighter by the minute, but something was strange, the sky was brighter higher up, the horizon was still dark. In the course of minutes everything became obvious: I was less than a mile from Montserrat, and the boat was drifting with northern current close to its western shore. It was strange, that I had not seen any lights of the Montserrat capital, Plymouth. Maybe I was too much to the east; Plymouth is located in the southwestern corner of the island, maybe it was obstructed by some promontory, maybe one of the frequent near shore rainy squalls had obstructed the lights, one way or another it was a close call.

I decided to enjoy the morning and prepared a hearty breakfast; during the night another flying fish had fallen into *Chatka,* yesterday's fish which was gutted and kept in a breezy place was also good.

The next day was pleasant sailing, wind about Force 3, small seas were hardly rocking the boat. I fastened the tiller, let the boat keep the course by herself, and in such a leisurely way I had passed the islands of Nevis, St. Christopher (also called St. Kitt), St. Eustatius, and finally, at the end of the day, Saba. Those two last islands are part of the Dutch West Indies; St. Eustatius was the base from which the Dutch were trading with the young United States during the War of Independence. The majority of big warehouses erected on that small island are now mostly underwater, because since those times a powerful earthquake caused considerable sinking of the shore.

After a night of easy sailing, the horizon was clear of any land, but not for long, because around noon St. Croix Island was visible, slightly to the port, and before nightfall the whole chain of the Virgin Islands was on the horizon. For the night I hove-to, a very easy maneuver for the boat that is ketch rigged, *Chatka* was lazily moving back and forward in short semicircles, barely changing her position during the night. With the first light the boat was again under way, and in a few hours I was at the entrance to the main harbor of St. Thomas, Charlotte Amalie.

Chatka Puchatków had a comfortable berth at the local yacht club, as usual, but nobody here knew anything about Wladek Wagner. Fortunately the Polish flag on my boat brought two Poles: a retired physicist and a young Polish woman, Ewa, who was living in Tortola, British Virgin Islands, with her British husband, Geoffrey. She was visiting Charlotte Amalie for some business and invited me to their house for a few days' stay in Tortola. The physicist was an extremely pleasant and knowledgeable gentleman who knew many interesting stories about Poland from her independence years between the First and Second World War, I spent hours listening with real interest. Neither he nor Ewa knew about Wagner's whereabouts, but Ewa promised me to find out more about him in Tortola. Her house was on the seashore, east from the capital Road Town, not far from Beef Island. She knew that an airport was being built on that little flat island, and that a short causeway and bridge were in place to link it with Tortola.

On a prearranged day a motorboat picked me up in a yacht club, Ewa and Geoffrey were waiting for me at the Road Town, and we drove to their beautiful house. Tortola has a very good climate, much nicer than, for example, Miami in South Florida. Winters are warmer and summers are cooler, but there was one problem: lack of fresh water. If I spent more than 30 seconds in a shower, for sure there would be banging on the door. Now there are two problems: lack of fresh water and a flood of tourists.

Returning to the Wagner pursuit: Ewa found out that he had sold Beef Island, hopefully with a profit, and had moved to Puerto Rico where he built a shipyard in Ponce-de-Leon, in the south of the island. I had not realized earlier that the big traffic of ocean going vessels in Charlotte Amalie had anything to do with cargo ships. The Virgin Islands did not produce much, and its small population did not consume much. Almost all the sea traffic consisted of passenger cruising vessels, bringing multitudes for shopping in a duty free harbor. There was nothing for me to do in Charlotte Amalie; it seemed that the next solitary sailing had to be to Puerto Rico, Wagner or no Wagner. I had to chase cargo shipping in order to bring *Chatka* to Europe. Therefore I decided to go to San Juan, a much bigger harbor than Ponce, I had enough money to spend for a bus ride to Ponce to meet this famous sailor.

The time I had spent with Ewa and Geoffrey was fabulous. I was an accomplished swimmer and diver, but rather a salvage kind of diver: if something was lost overboard I could free dive 12 meters (more than 39 feet) to retrieve a lost item. But it was in and out, half a minute dive into the cold and murky waters of the Baltic Sea. In Tortola I was introduced to snorkeling in crystal clear, tropical waters. In front of their house there was a huge natural pool connected to the sea, full of small fish, coral, sea urchins, marine vegetation. I could watch the action there for hours: baby barracudas ambushing tiny fish, small fish guarding their nests, and attacking much bigger trespassers, everything bathed in bright sunshine, making the colorful scene even more appealing.

Having decided to have a swim in that pool, I donned fins and a mask, attached a snorkel, waded into the pool. Lying on the surface, and looking through the mask, the view was even prettier. The water was incredibly clear, it was like floating in air, as a matter of fact I subconsciously behaved as if I was in the air. I took a shallow dive to be closer to something interesting on the bottom of the pool and kept breathing while going down. A lungful of salt water served as a rude awakening; coughing and spitting salt water, I rushed to shore. Soon I was back in the water, this time with my harpoon gun, the same one I had used to spear the mahi-mahi during our Atlantic passage. Fish, when viewed through the mask, appear to be much bigger than they are. I speared a sizeable one. Out of the water it looked small, just as it was. Geoffrey's comment was polite: "You must have a very good aim to be able to hit such a small target."

I was promised a real dive. Geoffrey, a seasoned diver, had some business with the family who lived on Salt Island, just across the Sir Francis Drake Channel, three or four miles from their home. We anchored in about 20 feet of water, near the shore not far off the western tip of the islet. We jumped in and, to my astonishment, I saw that below our boat was an enormous ship's propeller! Looking down a very steep slope I could see a huge wreck, its bows were disappearing in the blue depths. This time I was a spectator; Geoffrey dove beneath the stern of the wreck and brought up a big fish, weighing about 20 pounds. We loaded it into the boat and he dove again; this dive resulted in spearing a similar-sized fish, of a different kind. Those fish were intended to be the gift for a Salt Island family, one of the few living there; they had a few boats, few coconut palms, and plenty of children. The center of the islet consists of two large shallow lagoons; at the beginning of the dry season lagoons (locally called "ponds") are separated from the sea, and when they dry out salt is harvested.

I learned that the wreck on which we were diving was the *RMS (Royal Mail Steamship) Rhone,* sunk there during a hurricane in 1867, with a heavy loss of life. If somebody would like to find information about *Rhone* on the Internet at the present time, it would be difficult: any meaningful data is buried in hundreds of advertisements touting the dive services offering the underwater tours of *Rhone*. The remains of that 310-foot ship must be very crowded, days and nights, because nightly dives are also offered.

The ride back to St. Thomas was unpleasant, windy and rainy; this was the only day during my stay in the Virgin Islands when the weather was not perfect. Early the next morning, after returning from Tortola, *Chatka Puchatków* was on her way again, sailing in perfect weather towards Puerto Rico. Beautiful scenery, sheltered waters, fair wind, all those factors should add to a most pleasant time for everyone onboard. Unfortunately that was not the case. My course was leading me through waters requiring constant vigilance, very rarely could I leave the tiller to fix a meal, take bearings to fix exactly my position, or for whatever other reason. Of course I had expected this hardship and had prepared myself as well as I could for the rigors of a single-handed passage.

Soon after leaving Charlotte Amalie, a curious little islet named Sail Rock came into view, little to the starboard. When viewed from the east it looked like a two-masted sail ship, for sure the rock was aptly named. A few more hours and *Chatka* was skirting Culebra Island, part of the Commonwealth of Puerto Rico. During the late afternoon I sailed along the long line of the chain of low rocks named Cordillieras; those rocks shielded me from the Atlantic swell, as I left Palominos Island on my portside. Close to sundown, when small islets called Cucarachas replaced the Cordillieras, Cape San Juan, the north-eastern tip of the island of Puerto Rico was on my port beam, and I was sailing along the northern shore of that big island.

Port of San Juan was near, the water was deep, I relaxed a bit, the surf on the rocks of Punta Vacia Talega (Cap of Empty

Bag) startled me a little, I had to change course to slightly more offshore. My problem was that with the coming of darkness the wind slackened, and in order to enter the harbor I had to sail south, through the narrow entrance guarded by colonial fort El Morro. This fort is located on a high promontory forming the eastern shore of the passage into an extensive lagoon (locally called Bahia de San Juan). The current flows strongly to the west, and if I were to become becalmed on the lee of El Morro, *Chatka* could end up in the breaking swell of the western shore of the entrance. Therefore I was hugging the shore of Puerto Rico, maybe a little too close, but everything ended without any real danger. It is true that El Morro took whatever breeze was left, *Chatka* was drifting west, but using any breath of wind that was there from time to time, I managed safely my entrance into the lagoon; this trip took 16 hours. The city of San Juan was built on the strip of land between the Atlantic Ocean and a lagoon, its harbor is on the northern shore of the lagoon, which is long and shallow, extending far to the east. The yacht club (Club Nautico) is located in the eastern extremity, about 3 miles from the entrance; it took me 6 hours to finally reach my intended berth—just about sunrise.

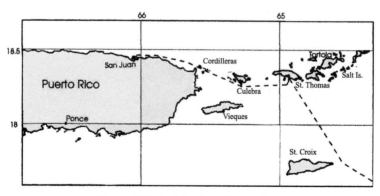

Chart of Virgin Islands to Puerto Rico.

After coming back to Poland this solitary trip (Martinique-San Juan), about 500 nautical miles, was touted as the longest solitary sail by a Polish sailor. It took some time before I learned that this opinion was erroneous—Jerzy Weber sailed alone from Tahiti to Palmerson Island, a distance of about 1,000 miles. That was in 1936, on the way he stopped in Bora Bora and Rarotonga, his yacht, *Farys,* was a few inches longer than 20 feet. He did not like solitary sailing either, from Palmerson Island to New Zealand he sailed with the help of an islander.

In recent decades, with navigation made easy by GPS and advances in communication, quite a few Poles have sailed long distances alone, even around the world, even by the difficult way of Cape Horn and Cape of Good Hope. Knowing my opinion of voluntary suffering, for sure you must realize that I am not envious.

15

Mr. Wagner—m/s Polanica—*Captain Konstanty Maciejewicz*—Chatka Puchatków *arrives in Gdynia.*

---

*A*FTER TWENTY-TWO HOURS of solitary sailing I was tired, of course. After securing *Chatka's* mooring lines and making a jury-rigged tent I went to sleep. Not for long, soon I had a visit from an immigration officer, he knew about our trip and was surprised that I was alone; he knew that originally there were two of us. Formalities took a few minutes; he radioed his nearby headquarters, which confirmed with St. Thomas that I had sailed alone.

I did not have to look for Mr. Wagner, somehow he had learned of my arrival and he showed up at Club Nautico early in the morning. His big yacht *s/y Rubicon* was moored nearby with a guard on board around the clock. He invited me to moor alongside his boat; at that time the yacht club in San Juan was not a secure place to leave a boat alone. As I have said *Rubicon* was a big boat, I do not remember her size exactly, but the thirty-foot long *Chatka* was very small compared to *Rubicon,* which must have been about 100 feet long. Previously she had belonged to the British Royal family and was built incredibly strong, with very good materials; for example, her planking was made of two-inch thick teak. Mr. Wagner was making some changes of the interior, and a considerable amount of the planking was exposed, I examined the beautiful wood very closely and could not find any knots or other imperfections.

I had a few dinners with Mr. Wagner, and his sailing stories were most interesting, sometimes incredible. His landfall after crossing the Atlantic in his *Zjawa* with two crewmen was north of the Brazilian Maraca Island. They did not have a dinghy, made a makeshift raft, left one of the crew on the anchored boat, and paddled three miles to shore. To their surprise, the shore consisted of a mangrove swamp, the rising sea breeze smashed the raft against the mangrove trees standing in water—it was high tide. They had spent the night in a tree, being bitten by hordes of mosquitoes; in the morning they lashed the saved remains of their raft, adding some dry mangrove branches and pushed it through the mangrove forest. Their intention was to use a much smaller raft as a float and, while swimming behind it, push it to the anchored *Zjawa*. The mangrove branches were denser than water and had to be cut off. With great difficulties, after many hours in the water, and already afternoon, they finally returned to their boat. That was my favorite story, Mr. Wagner's as well.[76]

Mr. Wagner was well known in the shipping circles and, without a problem, he arranged the transport of *Chatka* to New Orleans where she could be picked up by a Polish ship and delivered to Poland. It was arranged that I would wait in San Juan until a Polish ship arrived in New Orleans—often visited by the ships of the Polish Ocean Lines—then fly there and return to Gdynia onboard a Polish vessel.

I got the use of the *Rubicon's* dinghy; it was fitted with a small outboard engine, and I had a good time exploring the

---

[76] Wagner retired in Florida where, in 1987, he published the book about his voyage, *By the Sun and Stars*.

Bahia de San Juan, a lagoon of about 10 square miles. At that time there was a big seaplane naval base. It was interesting to see the antics of those mainly outdated planes that were used for training the pilots, mostly very inexperienced pilots.

Finally the Polish ship *m/s Polanica* was in New Orleans. I boarded the PANAM Clipper equipped with piston engines and after many hours landed in Miami. It was my first flight, quite memorable; we were flying above the chain of the Bahamas Islands, it was interesting to see them from far above. In Miami I changed to the National jet 707, it was my first flight on a jet plane. We landed when it was already night time; I was met by the immigration officer and escorted to *Polanica*. The trip to Poland took a few weeks. We took some cargo in Port Sulfur, Houston, and Galveston, then unloaded most of it in the West European harbors of La Pallice in France and Rotterdam in Holland.

Taking sulfur in Port Sulfur was an unpleasant experience; the fine yellow dust was everywhere, fortunately loading the stuff did not take much time—enormous conveyors did it in a few hours. Unloading it in Rotterdam was painless, it was sucked out, and the dust was on the other side, on the shore. La Pallice was, during the Second World War, an important German submarine base, massive bunkers with concrete roofs many feet thick were big enough for a number of submarines to moor inside for maintenance, taking in provisions and armament. This whole complex was practically untouched during the war, and it was possible to explore this very interesting site, especially for a sailor.

Crossing the Atlantic was unpleasant; *Polanica* was constructed in such a way that all machinery and the whole superstructure were located at the stern, therefore that's where most of the weight was located. Even when fully loaded, the front part of the ship was too light. It was July, and some remnants of a tropical disturbance gave us a sizeable swell. The big ship, when going close to the perpendicular to the seas, often had her front portion in the air. Seconds later, with a resounding bang it would crash into the water, making the whole boat shake violently.

Chatka Puchatków *on the deck of* m/s Oleśnica, *back in Gdynia.*

When it became known that I was on *Polanica,* I started to receive calls on the radiotelephone from many newspapers and press agencies. It was difficult to give interviews by radio, often connections were not the best, shore stations were cutting short our conversations.

That was just a prelude to all the attention I received after docking in Poland, in Gdynia; TV and radio interviews, and hundreds of articles in newspapers and magazines. In the beginning it was overwhelming, later it became boring. But there were pleasant moments: meeting with captains Meissner, Jurkiewicz, and Borchardt, who were interested in the professional part of the venture, as well as the writing of the accounts of our experiences in the professional paper *Ster.*[77] I received a call from the secretary of Captain Maciejewicz, the former director of the Maritime Academy. He had not seen me for many years, having been ousted from his position while I was on a tour on the square rigger *s/v Dar Pomorza* after my second year in the academy. Obviously, his ideology did not satisfy the powers to be; his replacement was a proper communist, whose sea knowledge was gained mostly by looking at pictures.

Captain Maciejewicz was requesting a meeting; for me it was a great honor. At the appointed time, after a handshake, he greeted me by: "Aha! Individualist!"[78] Then we had a very long chat, during which I had to answer a lot of probing questions about our trip. I think that we parted quite content with each other.

---

[77] *The Rudder.*

[78] For the benefit of Polish speakers: he said exactly "A! Indywidualista, znaczy sie!"

I spent a lot of time with Staszek Mioduszewski; together we made a number of public appearances. I spoke of the storms at sea, Staszek of the "storms" in the Polish press.

All that publicity had launched me on a lecture circuit, and when the communists vetoed another expedition I decided to study physics. My family was overjoyed; so far I was the only mature member of an extended family without a university degree. Five years later, when I received my master of science (physics)[79] degree, while visiting my parents after graduation, my mother had the idea to send a bunch of flowers with a thank-you note to the communist who was the leading force in stripping me of the right to practice my sailor profession and facilitated my decision to enter the Jagiellonian University in Krakow. I persuaded her that it would be a waste of money, better let's have a celebratory bottle of vodka. Everyone present had a drink to that.

It took a few more months for *Chatka Puchatków* to arrive in Gdynia. She was loaded in New Orleans on the deck of *m/s Oleśnica,* a sister ship of *Polanica*. She was placed, of all places, in the Museum of the Polish Navy. She was displayed there for more than twenty years. Just before the death rattle of the communist system in Poland, she was removed for maintenance. Soon after that Martial Law was declared, designed to save this odious and oppressive system in Poland. As we know, it did not work, now Poland is a democratic country; unfortunately, during the chaotic years of Martial Law, the boat was lost somewhere. It is a pity, not only because she was such a famous boat, but also because she was an

---

[79] In that time a masters was the highest degree that could be attained by study. To get a doctorate one had to produce some original research, usually after years of work.

example of a beautiful workmanship, produced at a time when the art of building wooden boats was in its peak and she was made of the highest quality materials.

Janusz was asked to try some novel design of a lifeboat built by one of the Polish shipyards; the idea was to sail her during the approaching storm and safely beach the boat on a sandy shore. Janusz completed his assignment perfectly; near the shore he "caught" the big wave and rode it far onto the beach. Because the heavy boat had sizeable momentum she moved forward even after her bottom was already touching the sand; the receding wave left her high and dry. The crew could leave the boat in total safety. I suspect that some communists' animosity towards me had rubbed off on Janusz; his feat was attacked in the official newspapers: all the expenses the government had to cover in order to dig a channel to launch the boat again!